In Search of the Absolute—essays on Swedenborg and Literature marks the third volume of a series of publications on Emanuel Swedenborg and his influence on the Arts and Humanities. The first volume, *Swedenborg and His Readers—essays by Dr John Chadwick*, examines his work within the cultural and linguistic context of the 18th century. The second, *On the True Philosopher and the True Philosophy*, looks more specifically at his influence on the history of Western philosophy. For information on future volumes please contact The Swedenborg Society, 20-21 Bloomsbury Way, London WC1A 2TH, England.

In Search of the Absolute—
Essays on Swedenborg and
Literature

In Search of the Absolute— Essays on Swedenborg and Literature

Edited and introduced by

Stephen McNeilly

Journal of the Swedenborg Society
Swedenborg House
20-21 Bloomsbury Way
London WC1A 2TH

—

2004

ACKNOWLEDGEMENTS

Many thanks to L Diaz Portal for her translation of Emilio R Báez-Rivera's
article 'Swedenborg and Borges: the Mystic of the North and the mystic *in Puribus*'.

Thanks also to John Elliott, Richard Lines, Paul McNeilly, Judith Portal Moreno and Lara
Muth for their help and comments.

Volume Three of the 'Journal of the Swedenborg Society'.

Enquiries concerning guidelines
for submission, editorial policy and information on future editions
should be directed to the Editor at the address below.

Editor: Stephen McNeilly
Assistant Editor: James Wilson

Published by:
The Swedenborg Society
Swedenborg House
20-21 Bloomsbury Way
London WC1A 2TH

Book design and artwork: Stephen McNeilly
Typeset at Swedenborg House.
Printed and bound in Great Britain at Biddles.

ISBN 0 85448 141 9
British Library Cataloguing-in-Publication Data.
A catalogue record for this book is available
from the British Library.

Table of Contents

| Contributors |

Emilio R Báez-Rivera is currently undertaking Doctoral Research at the University of Seville, Spain. In 1999, he was the winner of the Annual Literary Research Contest of the Academia Puertorriqueña de la Lengua Española, and the University of Puerto Rico's Presidential Scholarship in 2001. He was also awarded the Certificate of Advanced Studies in Latin American Literature at the University of Seville, Spain (2003). Research interests include the literature of Jorge Luis Borges, Saint Rosa of Lima, and the mystical writing of Latin American women. Previous articles include 'Del éxtasis a la palabra: retórica y hermetismo del discurso místico literario' (*Baple*, San Juan: Plaza Mayor, 1999).

Lars Bergquist is a novelist, essayist, translator and former Swedish ambassador to China and Italy. Among his many works published in Sweden are *Per brahes undergång och bärgning Isvandring med Nordenskiöld* and *Den heliga pyramiden*. He has also translated works into Swedish including Chinese Tang poetry and novels by Leonardo Sciascia. His English publications include Swedenborg's *Dream Diary* (Swedenborg Foundation, 2001). He has written a major biography of Swedenborg, entitled *Swedenborg's Secret*, soon to be published by the Swedenborg Society.

H J Jackson, a Professor of English at the University of Toronto, is the editor or co-editor of six volumes in the standard edition of Samuel Taylor Coleridge's *Collected Works*. She is also the editor of several trade editions of Coleridge and the author of *Marginalia: Readers Writing in Books* (Yale, 2001) and *A Book I Value* (Yale, 2003).

Anders Hallengren is an Associate Professor of Comparative Literature and a Research Fellow in the Department of History of Literature at Stockholm University. He is the Managing Editor of the literary journal *Parnass*. His publications include *The Puritan Mind and the Modern Self* (Guilin, 1989), *Deciphering Reality* (University of Minnesota, 1992), *The Code of Concord* (Almqvist & Wiksell International, 1994), *What is National Literature?* (Current History, 1996) and *A Gallery of Mirrors* (The Swedenborg Foundation, 1998).

Richard Lines is the Secretary of the Swedenborg Society. He has written a number of articles on Swedenborg's influence on literature, including 'Charles Augustus Tulk: Swedenborgian Extraordinary' (*Arcana*, Vol.III, No.4, Charleston, SC, 1997), 'The Inventions of William Blake, Painter and Poet: An Early Appreciation of Blake's Genius' (*The Journal of the Blake Society*, No 4, London, 1999) and 'James John Garth Wilkinson: Author, Physician and Translator' (*Annual Journal of the New Church Historical Society for the Year 2002*, Chester, 2002). He contributed an entry on Garth Wilkinson for *The Dictionary of Nineteenth-Century British Philosophers* (Thoemmes Press, 2002).

Stephen McNeilly lectures in Art and Critical Theory at the Kent Institute of Art and Design. He has edited a number of books including *x24: An Anthology of Contemporary Poetry* (Black Dog Press, 1997), *Swedenborg and His Readers—essays by Dr John Chadwick* (The Swedenborg Society, 2001), *On the True Philosopher and the True Philosophy* (The Swedenborg Society, 2002), *Introducing the Mystic* by Ralph Waldo Emerson (The Swedenborg Society, 2003) and *Introducing the New Jerusalem: Emanuel Swedenborg* (The Swedenborg Society, 2003).

Selected Works by Swedenborg

Listed chronologically

Published by Swedenborg

1709	Selected Sentences, (*Selectae Sententiae*).
1716	Northern Inventor, (*Daedalus Hyperboreus*).
1721	On Finding Longitude, (*Methodus Nova Inveniendi Longitudines Locorum Terra Marique Ope Lunae*).
	Principles of Chemistry, (*Prodromus Principiorum Rerum Naturalium, Sive Novorum Tentaminum Chymian et Physicam*).
1734	The Principia, or Principles of Natural Things, (*Principia Rerum Naturalium*).
	The Infinite and the Final Cause of Creation, (*Prodromus Philosophiae Ratiocinantis de Infinito, et Causa Finali Creationis*).
1740-42	The Economy of the Animal Kingdom, (*Oeconomia Regni Animalis*).
1744	The Animal Kingdom, (*Regnum Animale*).
1745	The Worship and Love of God, (*De Cultu et Amore Dei*).
1749-1756	Arcana Caelestia, (*Arcana Coelestia*).
1758	Earths in the Universe, (*De Telluribus in Mundo Nostri Solari*).
	Heaven and Hell, (*De Coelo et ejus Mirabilibus, et de Inferno*).
	The Last Judgment, (*De Ultimo Judicio*).
	The New Jerusalem and its Heavenly Doctrine, (*De Nova Hierosolyma*

---

et ejus Doctrina Coelesti).

The White Horse, *(De Equo Albo).*

1763   Doctrine of the New Jerusalem concerning the Lord, *(Doctrina Novae Hierosolymae de Domino).*

Doctrine of the New Jerusalem concerning the Sacred Scripture, *(Doctrina Novae Hierosolymae de Scriptura Sacra).*

Doctrine of Life for the New Jerusalem, *(Doctrina Vitae pro Nova Hierosolyma ex Praeceptis Decalogi).*

Doctrine of the New Jerusalem concerning Faith, *(Doctrina Novae Hierosolymae de Fide).*

Continuation of The Last Judgment, *(Continuatio de Ultimo Judicio).*

Divine Love and Wisdom, *(De Divino Amore et de Divina Sapientia).*

1764   Divine Providence, *(De Divina Providentia).*

1766   The Apocalypse Revealed, *(Apocalypsis Revelata).*

1768   Conjugial Love, *(De Amore Conjugiali).*

1769   Brief Exposition, *(Summaria Expositio Doctrinae Novae Ecclesiae).*

Interaction of the Soul and Body, *(De Commercio Animae et Corporis).*

1771   The True Christian Religion, *(Vera Christiana Religio).*

Published Posthumously

1719   On Tremulation, *(Anatomi af vår aldrafinaste natur, wisande att vårt rörande och lefwande wäsende består af contremiscentier).*

1734   Mechanism of the Soul and Body, *(De Mechanismo Animae et Corporis).*

1738-40   The Cerebrum, *(untitled MS).*

1739   Journeys 1710-1739, *(Itinerarium ex Annis).*

1742   Rational Psychology or The Soul, *(Psychologia Rationalis).*

Ontology, *(Ontologia).*

On Generation, *(De Generatione).*

1743-44	The Brain, (*De Cerebro*).
	The Journal of Dreams, (*Swedenborg's Drömmar*).
	A Philosopher 's Notebook, (*untitled MS*).
1744	Hieroglyphic Key, (*Clavis Hieroglyphica*).
	Correspondences and Representations, (*De Correspondentia et Representatione*).
1746-47	The Word Explained,(*Explicatio in Verbum Historicum Veteris Testamenti*).
	Index Biblicus,(*untitled MS*).
1747-1765	The Spiritual Diary, (*Diarium Spirituale*).
1757-1759	The Apocalypse Explained, (*Apocalypsis Explicata*).
1759	Athanasian Creed, (*De Athanasii Symbolo*).
1760	The Lord,(*De Domino*).
1761	Prophets and Psalms, (*Summaria Expositio Sensus Interni Librorum Propheticorum ac Psalmorum*).
	The Sacred Scripture or Word of the Lord, from Experience, (*De Scriptura Sacra seu Verbo Domini*).
1762	Precepts of the Decalogue, (*De Praeceptis Decalogi*).
	The Last Judgment Posthumous, (*De Ultimo Judicio Posth.*).
	The Divine Love, (*De Divino Amore*).
1763	The Divine Wisdom, (*De Divina Sapientia*).
1766	Conversations with Angels, (*Colloquia cum Angelis*).
	Charity, (*De Charitate*).
	Five Memorable Relations, (*Memorabilia*).
	Marriage, (*De Conjugio*).
1769	Canons of the New Church, (*Canones Novae Ecclesiae*).
	Scripture Confirmations, (*Dicta Probantia*).
	Index to Formula Concordiae, (*Index ad Formulam Concordiae*).
1770	Ecclesiastical History of the New Church, (*Historia Ecclesiatica Novae Ecclesiae*).
1771	Nine Questions, (*Quaestiones Novem de Trinitate*).

———

Reply to Ernesti, (*Responsum ad Dr Ernesti*).

Coronis, (*Coronis seu Appendix ad Veram Christianam Religionem*).

Consummation of the Age and Invitation to the New Church, (*De Consummatione Saeculi, de Adventu Secundo Domini*).

Fragment on Miracles, (*De Miraculis*).

Introduction

Stephen McNeilly

'When a person is prepared to receive the prophetical influx of correspond-ences', wrote Honoré de Balzac, in 1834, 'the spirit of the Word moves within him; he sees creation as a transformation; it gives vitality to his intellect, and a burning thirst for truth'.[1]

Balzac was 35 when he wrote this passage and, like William Blake before him, had already adapted Swedenborg's vast methodology into a personal system of symbols and signs. As Balzac rightly observes, the key to an understanding of Swedenborg's system lies in the notion of Correspondences. According to Swedenborg there is a symbolic relation between the world of nature and the divine that reveals itself at every instance of creation.[2]

There can be little doubt, today—given the rotary of names associated with his work—that Swedenborg's influence on the history of Western Literature is both far-reaching and varied. In addition to Balzac and Blake, we can find his name linked to the work of Johann Wolfgang von Goethe, Ralph Waldo Emerson, Samuel Taylor Coleridge, Thomas Carlyle, Robert and Elizabeth Barrett Browning, Joseph Sheridan Le Fanu, Alfred Tennyson, Paul Valéry, George MacDonald, Edgar Allen Poe, Walt Whitman, Fyodor Dostoyesky,

Arthur Conan Doyle, William Butler Yeats, Henry Miller, Jorge Luis Borges and Czeslaw Milosz. This list could go on.[3]

Indeed, it would be no exaggeration to suggest that without the writings of Swedenborg there would be no *Marriage of Heaven and Hell* (Blake), no 'Les correspondances' (Baudelaire), no *Inferno* (Strindberg) and no *Séraphita* (Balzac). There is even an entry reserved for Swedenborg in the subversive *Dictionnaire critique* of Georges Bataille.[4] 'We have come into a world that is a living poem', wrote Ralph Waldo Emerson in 1834, in an early attempt at defining this appeal:

> a poem that pierces the emblematic or spiritual nature of the visible, audible, tangible world.[5]

For Literary Criticism since, this 'poem' has come to represent one of the more enduring and yet illusive ideals of the 18th century. As Czeslaw Milosz wrote, in 1986, 'along with Dante and Blake...Swedenborg represents a decisive testimony to the imaginative life', an '*energy*' that only reveals itself in the constant interaction of the imagination with the five senses'.[6]

*

It is the aim of the essays collected here—beginning with Coleridge and closing with Borges—to shed greater light on this legacy and influence, showing the parallels of thought with writers and poets from the 19th century to the present day.

The first essay, by Professor H J Jackson, looks at one of the earliest readings of Swedenborg by the polymath of English Romanticism, Samuel Taylor Coleridge. She begins by discussing Coleridge's complex response to Swedenborg, and argues that, although Coleridge was often wary of Swedenborg's religious claims, he nevertheless took seriously the affinities between Swedenborg and other figures of the idealist tradition, most notably Plato and Schelling. In 1825, with the encouragement of the Swedenborgian Charles Augustus Tulk, he even went so far as to propose writing two volumes on Swedenborg; an essay on the 'Science of Correspondences' and 'A History of the Mind of

Swedenborg'. It was Charles Augustus Tulk, in turn, who first introduced Coleridge to William Blake.

The second paper, by Professor Anders Hallengren, and continuing an exploration of the 19th century, looks at Swedenborg's influence on the work of Ralph Waldo Emerson. According to Professor Hallengren, Emerson (like Coleridge) makes use of the Science of Correspondences as a way of symbolically encoding moral and ethical values. Emerson's interest in Swedenborg, as such—and of American literature in general—involves the manner by which this system was utilised in an attempt to combine the truths of scientific discourses with literature and its use of imagination and beauty. Such a reading can be seen in Emerson's unique blending of aesthetics and ethics as found in his later essays, 'Self-reliance' and others.

The third article, by Richard Lines, focuses more closely on the specific influence of Swedenborg's *Conjugial Love*. Re-introducing the figure of Charles Augustus Tulk, Lines suggests that Swedenborg's book on marital love was introduced to Robert and Elizabeth Browning around 1848, and can be seen in Elizabeth's monumental *Aurora Leigh* and Robert's volume of poems *Men and Women*. From this date, he argues, one can find numerous (and largely unnoted) references to Swedenborg in their letters and poems. He also points to the influence of Swedenborg's *Conjugial Love* on the poetry of Coventry Patmore and Alfred Tennyson.

Anders Hallengren, in his second contribution to the volume, returns to the theme of American literature and a previously uncommented link with the poetry of Walt Whitman. Professor Hallengren draws our attention to an article by Whitman, in which he enthusiastically describes Swedenborg as a 'precursor', the link between the previous 'thousand years' and the future 'thousand years'. Professor Hallengren goes on to outline the Correspondential links between Whitman and Swedenborg in *Leaves of Grass*, and shows that early supporters of Whitman were also readers of Swedenborg.

The final two essays consider more recent interpretations of Swedenborg's thought. Lars Bergquist begins with an exploration of the later plays of August Strindberg and the transition of his work as marked in the 'Inferno Crisis' of 1894-96. Bergquist shows how Strindberg, following Emerson's reading of Swedenborg, saw Swedenborg as a 'teacher and guide' in the 'sea of the world of visions'. Drawing on Swedenborg's conception of man as a constantly creative being, Strindberg outlines his own version of Correspondences. The specific examples drawn to here are *A Dream Play*, *To Damacus* and *The Blue Books*.

The final article, by Emilio R Báez-Rivera, closes with a comparison of the mystical experiences of Swedenborg with the literature of Jorge Luis Borges. Báez-Rivera claims that Borges himself underwent two mystical experiences. These experiences not only informed his writing but led him to regard Swedenborg as one of the greatest of mystics. Borges' interest is revealed in two short essays published as biographical notes, and a lecture in which he describes Swedenborg's style as a 'serene prose...lucid, and without metaphor or exaggeration'. Like the short story 'The Aleph' and his essay 'A New Refutation of Time' one can see a vindication of the authenticity of Swedenborg's mysticism through Borges' discussion of the dissolution of space and time. In both cases, argues Báez-Rivera, Borges unfolds a mystical system in which the methodology of Swedenborg is offered as both a guiding thread and framework. Swedenborg will continue to interest us, argues Borges, because his writings offer us a mirror in which we are constantly reminded of the symbolic value of things.

NOTES

[1] Honoré de Balzac, *Séraphita*, translated by Clara Bell, (Dedalus, 1989), 62. The passage cited here has been gently revised.

[2] For a full account of Swedenborg's Science of Correspondences see his *Heaven and Hell* §§87-140. In a most general sense this Science might be understood as follows:

According to Swedenborg there is a correspondential link between man, nature and the Divine. All of our thoughts, affections and emotions—in fact everything about us, both physical and non-physical—are mirrored in the Divine, and by degrees, in nature. On one level, this means that the objects encountered in the physical world, i.e., animals, plants, rocks, heat, cold, space and time, are actual manifestations of the same impulses that give rise to our own desires and thoughts. The parasite exists in nature, and we recognise it as such, argues Swedenborg because it mirrors the selfish and myopic nature within ourselves and others, as does the lamb with our innocence. This innocence, in turn, can only exist within us because it first exists within God and the parasite exists because it represents the corruption of this innocence, via free will.

Language plays a unique role in this relation, argues Swedenborg, because the written word—through its dependence on symbols, metaphors and relations—is already self-evidently balanced between the world of things and the world of thoughts. It is this very balance, in fact, that offers it a privileged space for the 'divine breath' or divine animation. For Swedenborg, Sacred Scripture is the 'blue print' or 'key' to the divine itself, which he explains in his *Arcana Caelestia*, *The Apocalypse Explained* and *The Apocalypse Revealed*. The difference between Swedenborg and other traditions asserting a symbolic link between man and God, therefore, is that for Swedenborg the link between man, nature and the divine is not *merely* symbolic but *essentially* symbolic.

[3] More recently we can find Swedenborg's name cited by writers as diverse as Italo Calvino, Peter Ackroyd and A S Byatt.

[4] Georges Bataille, *Encyclopædia Acephalica*, edited by R Lebel and I Waldberg, (Atlas Books, 1997). The entry in question comes under the heading of 'Angel' and offers a lengthy quotation from Swedenborg's *Heaven and Hell*.

[5] Ralph Waldo Emerson, *The Complete Works of Ralph Waldo Emerson,* (Boston and New York, 1904), IV, 115f.

[6] Czeslaw Milosz, 'Dostoyesky and Swedenborg', published in *Testimony to the Invisible: Essays on Swedenborg*, edited by J F Lawrence (The Swedenborg Foundation, 1995).

In Search of the Absolute—
Essays on Swedenborg and
Literature

'Swedenborg's *Meaning* is the truth': Coleridge, Tulk, and Swedenborg

H J Jackson

C oleridge was born in 1772, the year of Swedenborg's death. He must have been aware in a general way of the nature of Swedenborg's work and the rapid spread of his influence in England, but it was not until 1817, when he met Charles Augustus Tulk, that he undertook a careful study of the writings of Swedenborg and became for a short time involved in the business of the Swedenborg Society. At one point he gleefully reported to Tulk the rumour that he had experienced a religious conversion: "They say, Coleridge! that you are a Swedenborgian!".[1] But they both knew that it was not true. Coleridge turned 45 in 1817, Tulk 31. Though Swedenborg himself is proof that conversion may occur late in life, Coleridge was not converted by reading his work. He cannot even be properly said to have been *influenced* by Swedenborg, though he was certainly interested by him and consistently described him as a man of 'philosophic Genius'.[2] Since Coleridge came to a knowledge of Swedenborg through Tulk and since many of his statements about Swedenborg and the New Church were directly or indirectly addressed to Tulk, I want to begin by briefly retelling the story of the relationship between them before considering the nature and evolution of Coleridge's own involvement with the Swedenborgian movement.

At the time when they met (on holiday at the seaside), both men were about as pros-perous and contented as they would ever be. Tulk, with a large fortune, had been happily married for ten years and had a growing family to care for. As a founder member of the Swedenborg Society, then known as the 'Society for Printing and Publishing the Writings of the Hon. Emanuel Swedenborg, instituted in London in the Year 1810', he continued a family tradition (his father, John Augustus, had been involved in the original Theosophical Society of 1783 and took an active part in the new one) and was kept busy in a good cause. He helped to organize the publication and distribution of Swedenborg's works, contributed articles to the New Church *Intellectual Repository*, chaired sessions of the Society and of the Hawkstone Meeting, and did some translating himself. As to Coleridge, he was enjoying the sheltered harbour of a surgeon's family after twenty turbulent and troubled years. Under the Gillmans' care in Highgate he had reduced his dependency on opium to a controlled dose and, thus stabilised, seemed to be picking up the pieces of his literary career. In 1816-17 he had published 'Christabel' and 'Kubla Khan', brought out an autobiography and a volume of collected poems, and contributed two 'Lay Sermons' to the current political debates. He had in the works an introduction to an encyclopedia (the 'Treatise on Method'), a three-volume revised version of his periodical *The Friend*, and an annotated selection from the works of the seventeenth-century Archbishop of Glasgow, Robert Leighton. Shortly after meeting Tulk, he began to work regularly with a young surgeon and Germanist, Joseph Henry Green, with the aim of articulating a coherent system of philosophy to displace both Newtonian materialism and post-Kantian idealism.[3]

In the period of their *close* friendship, which lasted about ten years, Tulk's and Coleridge's circumstances naturally changed. Coleridge delivered public lectures and privately gave lessons in philosophy, but was often ill. Tulk had the satisfaction of serving for six years as a Member of Parliament, but he suffered the loss of his wife Susanna in 1824 and never remarried. (Coleridge did not handle the death well: though he later said that he had written as soon as he heard the news, he did not post his letter and Tulk had to write to him some months later to find out what had happened.[4]) Realising that they had a good deal in common, they put considerable effort into reinforcing the ties between them. In 1818 they both campaigned for better conditions for children working in the cotton factories. Tulk attended some of Coleridge's lectures, and probably mentioned them to other friends—Coleridge sent him copies of the prospectus. He assisted and advised Coleridge in difficult negotiations with the publisher John Murray. Coleridge and Gillman in turn advised him in his attempt to buy a house near them in Highgate after the death of his wife.[5]

In all these practical matters Coleridge and Tulk did what they could to support one another. But the basis of their intimacy was an intellectual affinity that had been apparent from the very beginning. Coleridge knew no half measures in friendship: he registered his excitement over meeting a kindred spirit by sending Tulk two whopping letters outlining his system of dynamic philosophy.[6] Tulk responded by lending and giving Coleridge books. The first we hear of are titles that might have been expected to appeal to Coleridge's poetic and philosophic tastes while also having connections with Swedenborg: Blake's *Songs of Innocence and of Experience*, some work of Schelling's, an Indian poem and notes on Spinoza.[7] By October 1819, Tulk had Coleridge reading Swedenborg's own works, both theological and scientific. They must have eagerly talked over Swedenborg's philosophy and theology when they had the opportunity, continuing the discussion in letters when they were apart. In January 1820, Coleridge wrote:

> If I mistake not, one formula would comprise your philosophical faith & mine—namely, that the sensible World is but the evolution of the Truth, Love, and Life, or their opposites, in Man—and that in Nature Man beholds only (to use an Algebraic but close analogy) the integration of Products, the Differentials of which are in, and constitute, his own mind and soul—and consequently that all true science is contained in the Lore of Symbols & Correspondences.[8]

Tulk sometimes rode up to Highgate, Coleridge sometimes went to stay with the Tulks for a few days. Coleridge's excitement about what he was reading spilled over in the form of literary projects.

Knowing Tulk's responsibilities, Coleridge proposed several publishing ventures for the Society, in some of which he was prepared to be personally involved. Since he considered Swedenborg to be 'illustrious tho' grossly misconceived', he made memoranda in the pages of his Latin copy of *Heaven and Hell* about ways in which the followers of Swedenborg might prevent misunderstanding in the future:

> But again I repeat my conviction, that Swedenborg's *Meaning* is the truth—and the duty of his followers is, to secure this meaning to the Readers of his Works by collecting from his numerous Volumes those passages, in which this meaning is conveyed in terms so plain as not to be misconceived: an Introduction of 50 pages would suffice for this purpose.[9]

At the annual meeting of the Society in 1817, Tulk had been able to remind members of the Society that they had achieved a major part of the purpose for which they had joined together, namely the translation and publication of all the 'divinely illuminated writings' of Swedenborg, and that they were now embarked on second editions and new translations.[10] Coleridge's letters to Tulk suggest another direction that the Society might choose to pursue. The works were out, to be sure, but they were misunderstood; by judicious presentation, adapting the works for a nineteenth-century British readership, the Society could see to it that they were correctly understood—or, as we might put it, could attempt to control interpretation. Further suggestions in the 1820s included an octavo companion volume to *The True Christian Religion*, a blank-verse version of *Conjugial Love*, an '*introductory* Essay to the Science of Correspondences', and 'a history of the mind of Swedenborg'. The last of these Tulk is said actually to have proposed to the Society in 1825, recommending a commission of £200. The offer was rejected, allegedly because of doubts about Coleridge's doctrinal fitness for the task.[11] From the point of view of the Church, if not of Tulk, those doubts were well founded.

The survival of many of Coleridge's notebooks and annotated books, as well as a substantial portion of his side of the correspondence with Tulk, means that it is possible to trace the history of his views about Swedenborg in detail, only bearing in mind that his comments must often have been coloured by his desire to please his friend. When Coleridge said that Swedenborg had been 'grossly misconceived', he could have been describing his own situation, for he had himself misconceived Swedenborg. Before meeting Tulk, he was aware that Swedenborg had described visions of heaven and hell; he knew about the controversies surrounding the establishment of the New Jerusalem Church; and he had read some of the major critics of Swedenborgianism, certainly Kant and probably Wesley and Priestley.[12] He shared the common prejudices of his day and age and church against Swedenborg, as we can see by a couple of throwaway remarks made at some distance before and after his period of sympathetic engagement in the early 1820s. In a lecture of 1808 he referred to 'Mahometanism which is only an anomalous corruption of Christianity, like Swedenborgianism', and in a notebook entry of 1833 about the meaning of the Old Testament prophecies he asks, 'May we dare hope for a *sane* Swedenborg?'[13] It seems that his unguarded opinion, to the end of his life, was that Swedenborg was in some sense mad, and that the church founded in his name was misguided. In 1826, describing Tulk for the benefit of another friend who was about to meet him, he expressed his pleasure in the fact that Tulk was a non-sectarian Swedenborgian who chose, like other leaders of the movement from the early years and like Swedenborg himself, to remain a member of the established Church.[14] But Coleridge vacillated between trying to conform to contemporary society, and to reform it. Attacked for obscurity and Germanic mysticism himself, he was cautious about having his name publicly connected with the Swedenborgians and avoided any positive endorsement in his published works.[15]

On the other hand, in a strange sequence of notebook entries dating from very early in Coleridge's career, a series that includes recipes, addresses, extracts from books, noteworthy jokes, and ideas for new poems and publishing projects, we encounter 'Mem. To reduce to a regular form the Swedenborgian's Reveries'.[16] (Not Swedenborg's, but the Swedenborgian's.) It is impossible to say exactly what Coleridge can have had in mind; the immediate context of the notebooks offers no help. But the idea, however sketchy, would be consistent with Coleridge's lifelong interest in dreams and dreamlike states, his conviction that they were meaningful, and his efforts to 'reduce' them to an intelligible order. If at one level of thought he was disposed to downplay the effect of Swedenborg's visions, at another he was aware of their power. Some of the latest references to Swedenborg in his letters and notebooks are allusions to those parts of *Heaven and Hell* (probably §§ 576-88) that describe the plurality of hells and of demons. Coleridge ruefully imagines gastric devils in his own insides, bringing him terrible dreams——'a woeful passage for me that in the Honorable Baron's Visa et Audita: for it has haunted me ever since I first read it, and *in my Sleep* I believe or at least take it for granted'.[17] The imagery of *Heaven and Hell* evidently had a lasting effect even if its doctrine did not; and this is ironical given Coleridge's conscious reservations about the imagery and his intuitive receptivity to the doctrine.

Another image that Coleridge found particularly resonant, that is associated with a warm tribute to Swedenborg and that may therefore have been prompted by *Conjugial Love* although it also has solid Platonic credentials, is the image of the androgyne, which occurs in a passage in the *Notebooks* that Virginia Woolf later made famous. Coleridge is observing that great minds often go together with unassertive manners:

> The truth is, a great mind must be *androgyne*. Great minds (Swedenborg's for instance) never wrong but in consequence of being in the right—tho' imperfectly. Such was the case with his adherence to the mechanic philosophy, even to the last— as in his notion of the human Will being placed in the *punct*[*um*] *indifferentiae* between the Heavens & the Hells——[18]

Thus Swedenborg may have contributed obliquely, through Coleridge, to the formation of a controversial concept of modern feminism.

In order to disentangle the various strands of Coleridge's ambivalent response, it is necessary to consider his comments on Swedenborg in relation to his philosophy at large. In the 1820s he was trying to work out a comprehensive philosophical system to combat what he saw as the prevailing complacent materialism of his time. He aimed to incorporate whatever was valid from other systems, going by the Leibnizian axiom that most parties in philosophy have some apprehension of the truth, and that a 'true philosophy' would 'collect the fragments of truth scattered through systems apparently the most incongruous'.[19] Another mantra for him, however, was that a partial truth could do as much damage as outright falsehood. In the *Lay Sermons* of 1816 he had declared that 'If we are a christian nation, we must learn to act nationally, as well as individually, as Christians. We must remove half-truths, the most dangerous of errors...by the whole Truth.'[20] So as he read Swedenborg, he struggled to separate wheat from chaff, in order to adopt or adapt what was valuable in a more nearly perfect philosophical whole.

Reading Swedenborg for effectively the first time, Coleridge was struck by the affinities between Swedenborg's ideas and values and those of other eminent but marginalised thinkers in an idealist and mystical tradition that extended from Plato to Schelling. Where we might be inclined to see common sources and influences, Coleridge believed he was seeing recurrent glimpses, scattered fragments as he would say, of an ultimate truth, confirmed by their reappearance in writers and visionaries remote from one another in time or place—indeed, the more remote the better. Singularity was no recommendation. Coleridge likened Swedenborg to a distinguished and, on the face of it, discordant host: to Plotinus, Porphyry, Augustine, Aquinas, Duns Scotus, Luther, Pico della Mirandola, Giordano Bruno, Böhme, George Fox, Spinoza, and recent German philosophers of nature—Schelling, Schubert and Eschenmayer. What do they have in common? Well, not much—or rather, no one thing, but a family resemblance. Some of them were system-makers, some interpreters, some millenarians, some visionaries. Some of them advocated a new way of reading the Bible; some declared the humanity of God and the divinity of humanity; some taught the immateriality of the natural world and the reality of the spiritual world. Most of them were misfits either in their own time or in the world that Coleridge knew, and he revered them as heroic representatives of an alternative world-view even though he thought their formulations were incomplete or otherwise flawed. In *Biographia Literaria*, published just before he met Tulk, he had eloquently attacked the prejudice against 'enthusiasts' like Fox and Böhme, and gratefully acknowledged their role in his own intellectual development: 'they contrived,' he said, 'to keep alive the *heart* in the *head*'.[21] Coleridge kept a little list of 'revolutionary minds' that he wanted to write about in a 'Vindication of great men unjustly branded', and Swedenborg's name was soon added to it.[22]

Coleridge found much to admire in Swedenborg as a fellow warrior in the battle against philosophical materialism. On key topics he seemed to be on the right side, his insights strengthened, to Coleridge's mind, by their appearing to coincide with and thus to confirm the formulations of figures such as Plotinus, Augustine, Luther, and Böhme (which in turn acted to confirm his). He admired the coherence and comprehensiveness of the system itself, which explained the external, natural world as a product of the internal world of spirit. He acknowledged that Swedenborg's science was ahead of its time and that 'Much of what is most valuable in the physiosophic works of Schelling, Schubert, and Eschenmayer is to be found anticipated in this supposed *Dementato*'.[23] He thought that along with Luther and the Moravians, Swedenborg had got the crucial doctrine of the Logos right: the Logos was to be sought and found in 'the divine Humanity'.[24] He noted affinities between Swedenborg's three worlds and the threefold vision of Augustine and the neo-Platonists:

> Augustine teaches the same doctrine as Swedenborg: there can be but three essentially different Genera of Being—Divine, Human, and Bestial. And Reason says the same/ The absolute rational, the finite Rational, and the Irrational—or 1. the Absolute. 2. the rational Finite. 3. the irrational Finite. God, Man, and nature exhaust our conception.[25]

He applauded the Doctrine of Correspondences and the project of interpreting the Bible in a consistently spiritual sense. In a notebook entry of 1827 concerned chiefly with the prophetic books of the Old Testament and their relationship to Christian doctrine, he rather wistfully raised the possibility of an unbroken but unwritten tradition of interpretation in 'an interior and spiritual sense...still discoverable by a spiritual Light', which he said he would seize on if he could only 'be sure, it was more than an Opinion./ The invidious epithets of Swedenborgian and Cabalistic, would not frighten me'.[26]

But Swedenborg also in many ways made Coleridge very uneasy and no positive comment comes without reservations. There were serious divergences between them on certain theological issues: Swedenborg, for instance, firmly rejected the doctrine of the Trinity of persons. Coleridge was still more at odds with Swedenborg's New Church followers, whom he accused of being materialists at heart: 'the Letter hideth the spirit from them. As they read, so they believe—both with the eyes of the body...For such men it is either literal or metaphorical. There is no third. For to the *Symbolical* they have not arrived'.[27] But the most important differences between him and Swedenborg were not isolated but systemic, and the root of Coleridge's objections was the way that the Swedenborgian system depended on Swedenborg's visions of angels. It was not that he took Swedenborg for a charlatan or fantasist or madman, as many of his contemporaries did. He never doubted that Swedenborg had had the experiences he described. But since his visions could not be corroborated by any second witness or any further evidence, there was the distinct risk that they might be altogether subjective and idiosyncratic. Comparing the visions of Swedenborg with the vision that converted St Paul, Coleridge pointed out that in Paul's case, there had been objective evidence in the form of a miracle in addition to his subjective experience: 'N.B. Not every revelation requires a sensible Miracle as the credential—but every Revelation of a *new* series of Credenda [does]'.[28] Worse, by representing the spirit world in distinctly physical terms, Swedenborg's account seemed to contradict itself: what could be seen and heard, if not held and touched, was not immaterial enough for Coleridge. Such appeals to the senses, he thought, were liable to lead to idolatry and pantheism.[29]

Coleridge tried by various means to salvage Swedenborg's 'meaning', which was 'truth', from the humanly flawed form in which it was embodied. His interpretative strategies can be seen most clearly in marginalia to three Swedenborgian books, the Latin copy of *Heaven and Hell* (*De Coelo...et de inferno, ex auditis et visis*); *The True Christian Religion*; and Samuel Noble's 1826 defence of the New Church, *An Appeal on behalf of the Views of the Eternal World and State, [etc.]*. (Though these books were his own property, Coleridge's library circulated freely and he knew other people would see the marginalia. He made a diplomatic effort to soften the criticism in one set of notes by observing, for the sake of 'any other eyes, but my own' that might see them, that his disagreement could well be no more than a misunderstanding arising from the lack of definitions of key terms.[30]) In his notes, Coleridge paid Swedenborg the tribute of subjecting his work to the kinds of tests that biblical scholarship was then applying to the 'inspired' writings of the Old and New Testaments. Were they internally consistent? Were they susceptible of a symbolical as well as a literal reading? Were they in harmony with the rest of the canon? How were essential doctrines to be purged of the accidental details of historical and cultural context?

On the vexed question of the visions themselves, Coleridge tried out a number of approaches. He found a ready physiological explanation for Swedenborg's experiences in new theories of mesmerism (also known as animal magnetism or zoomagnetism) which would not have been available in Swedenborg's day. Using mesmeric terminology, Coleridge repeatedly describes Swedenborg as a 'clairvoyant' or 'somnambulist'.[31] The same or a similarly rare organic condition might account, he thought, for the *forms taken* by the quite different visions of other mystics. Believers were not obliged to accept the form along with the substance of the belief. The angelic figures could therefore be dispensed with as idiosyncratic elements in the system—they were, as Coleridge puts it, not objectively subjective but individually subjective.[32] Instead of 'regarding the System as the Relation of actual Travels', therefore, the respectful reader 'would receive it as the Account of a Series of allegorical in part & in part symbolical Visions, some of which the gifted Seer had misinterpreted'.[33] It may be some mitigation of Coleridge's presumptuousness (maintaining that Swedenborg did not know what he was saying while he, Coleridge, did) to remember that he would have said the same of the prophets of the Old Testament and the Evangelists of the New, and would expect to have it said of himself by more advanced thinkers in the course of time.

Even if the physiological explanation were not correct, and Swedenborg's visions were genuine supernatural visitations, still acceptance of the truth of the whole system of belief must depend, Coleridge pointed out, on its compatibility with 'the Light of the Eternal and of the Written Word—i.e. with the Scriptures and with the sciential and the practical Reason'.[34] It had to be systematic (logically consistent) and scripturally sound. Coleridge complained that the system was not internally coherent and not immaterial enough, but when he tried to dematerialise it and to make it coherent, he tended to produce unappealing paraphrases, starting off with a formula such as 'Now if I understand Sw. aright, he means...'.[35] For the concrete particulars of Swedenborg's vivid encounters with God and the angels, for example, Coleridge substituted abstract propositions:

> The Transgression consists not in the sort of Image, nor whether one Image or three, but in presenting any image at all, either to the bodily or mental Eye...All therefore [that] Swedenborg meant or could mean, is this—Suppose for a moment what is not however the possible subject of a rational Supposition, that the Deity could *appear totally*, or indeed *appear* at all as God—then it would be deducible ...that the Deity would appear in the Human Form.[36]

Coleridge plainly struggled to translate the details of Swedenborg's system of belief into terms compatible with one that he found more inclusive and more universally applicable. He wanted Swedenborg's work to be less naturalistic and more rigorous, to bring it into line with what he regarded as the best thought from Plato to Kant. He thought it would benefit from a regular appeal to first principles, and from a stricter definition of terms.[37] But then the system would no longer be Swedenborg's, as becomes strikingly evident when Coleridge claims that Swedenborg could not have meant what he said about the doctrine of justification by faith, and has to over-ride Swedenborg's explicit rejection in order to reconcile his thinking with that of Luther and 'the Founders & Fathers of the Church of Christ in England'.[38] In a well-meant, for the period broad-minded, but ultimately patronizing way, Coleridge tried to make Swedenborg over as a systematic philosopher, one of the special set of '*Christian* Philosophers' to which he declared he and Tulk belonged.[39]

Coleridge had a history of keen engagement with one new friend after another, most of these relationships going up in smoke sooner or later, vanishing altogether or leaving only a charred shell to go on with. Southey and Wordsworth are the classic cases. But a few faithful figures, perhaps less competitive or more easy-going in the first place, survived the flames. Lamb, Green, and Gillman belonged to this group, and so did Tulk. He was certainly hurt by Coleridge's neglect of him after his wife's death, but they patched things up and continued to see one another. I venture to suggest that something of the same kind happened in Coleridge's relationships with books and ideas, and that the experience of enthusiasm followed by difficulties and disenchantment is not uncommon among us. Coleridge and Tulk knew what they could count on from one another; Coleridge in the end kept Swedenborg at a respectful distance. Still, a new opportunity could bring out a considered tribute, as in Coleridge's last note to Noble's *Appeal*, in 1827:

> I can venture to assert, that as a *moralist*, Swedenborg is above all praise; and that as a Naturalist, Psychologist, and Theologian he has strong and varied claims on the gratitude and admiration of the professional and philosophical Faculties.[40]

NOTES
  [1] S T Coleridge, *Letters*, ed. Earl Leslie Griggs, (Oxford, Clarendon Press, 1956-71), V, 136.
  [2] E.g., S T Coleridge, *Marginalia*, ed. H J Jackson and George Whalley, (Princeton, Princeton University Press, 1980-2001), V, 427, 444.

[3] The manuscript that they produced between them, the *Opus Maximum*, has just been published (2002) as the final volume of the standard edition of Coleridge's *Collected Works*. Green's version of their system was published shortly after his death as *Spiritual Philosophy*, a title tellingly close to that of Tulk's magnum opus, *Spiritual Christianity*.

[4] Coleridge, *Letters*, V, 420.

[5] Coleridge, *Letters*, IV, 841-4, 883-4, 914-15; V, 281-4, 291-3; VI, 605-20. Both sets of negotiations were ultimately unsuccessful.

[6] Coleridge, *Letters*, IV, 767-76, 804-9.

[7] Coleridge, *Letters*, IV, 835-8, 883-4.

[8] Coleridge, *Letters*, V, 19.

[9] Coleridge, *Letters*, V, 17; *Marginalia*, V, 410.

[10] Society for Printing and Publishing the Writings of The Hon. Emanuel Swedenborg, *Report of the Eighth Annual Meeting*, (London, 1817), 7.

[11] Coleridge, *Letters*, V, 174-5, 284, 327, 89n. The published minutes of the 1825 annual meeting, however, contain no reference to this offer.

[12] There exist three copies of Kant's *Vermischte Schriften* annotated by Coleridge, all with notes on Kant's attack on Swedenborg, *Träume eines Geistersehers*: Coleridge, *Marginalia*, III, 317, 333, 350-3. (His last word on Kant's opinion, in a note of about 1824, is a very strange psychological interpretation which accounts for Kant's vehemence by supposing that he had been at first impressed by Swedenborg and inclined to believe in him, but subsequently disappointed in his works—an idea for which there is no external validation or corroboration of any kind, and which appears to be a projection of Coleridge's own experience.) As a young man Coleridge had been a great admirer of Priestley and followed his theological debates closely. If he did not actually read his 1791 *Letter to the New Jerusalem Church*, he must have known it by report: his sense of the issues raised by Swedenborg and the way to approach them matches Priestley's point by point. Wesley dismissed Swedenborg as a madman, as Coleridge could have known from his *Journal* or from various biographies that appeared after Wesley's death in 1791.

[13] Coleridge, *Lectures 1808-1819 on Literature*, ed. R A Foakes, (Princeton, Princeton University Press, 1987), I, 53; and *Notebooks*, ed. Kathleen Coburn and Anthony John Harding, (Princeton, Princeton University Press, 1957-2002), V, #6764.

[14] Coleridge, *Letters*, VI, 583-4.

[15] Coleridge, *Letters*, V, 284. He was plainly nettled by a review of December 1820 that associated him with Böhme and Swedenborg, i.e., in the opinion of the reviewer, with incomprehensible mystics: *Letters*, V, 125. In the 1818 revised edition of *The Friend* he had offered a hedged or back-handed compliment—about as close as he ever came to public endorsement. There he says that in any system of belief that becomes widely diffused there is bound to be a measure of truth. Even of such apparently far-fetched ideas as the doctrine 'of a latent mystical sense in

the words of Scripture and the works of nature, according to Emanuel Swedenborg', which might well be 'a distorted and dangerous, as well as partial, representation of the truth, on which it is founded...I dare, and do, affirm that it always does shadow out some important truth': *Friend*, ed. Barbara Rooke, (Princeton, Princeton University Press, 1969), I, 430.

[16] Coleridge, *Notebooks*, I, #165, (dated 1796).

[17] Coleridge, *Notebooks*, V, #5640, (1827). See also *Notebooks*, IV, 5460; *Letters*, V, 216, 388, 489, and VI, 607.

[18] Coleridge, *Notebooks*, IV, #4705. Virginia Woolf refers to the passage in *A Room of One's Own*, (London, Grafton, 1977; rpt 1987), 93-4.

[19] Coleridge, *Biographia Literaria*, ed. James Engell and W Jackson Bate (Princeton, Princeton University Press, 1983), I, 247, 244.

[20] Coleridge, *Lay Sermons*, ed. R J White, (Princeton, Princeton University Press, 1972), 288.

[21] Coleridge, *Biographia Literaria*, I, 152. An important related passage appears in *Shorter Works and Fragments*, II, 829-30.

[22] Coleridge, *Marginalia*, III, 990-1; also *Shorter Works and Fragments*, Ed. H J Jackson and J R de J Jackson, (Princeton, Princeton University Press, 1995), I, 770.

[23] Coleridge, *Marginalia,* V, 427.

[24] Coleridge, *Notebooks*, IV, 4671.

[25] Coleridge, *Marginalia*, III, 985.

[26] Coleridge, *Notebooks,* V, #5667.

[27] Coleridge, *Letters*, V, 91.

[28] Coleridge, *Marginalia*, V, 987.

[29] Coleridge, *Marginalia*, V, 406.

[30] Coleridge, *Marginalia*, V, 409.

[31] E.g., in *Marginalia*, III, 353; V, 467; *Notebooks*, IV, #4908 fol. 68.

[32] Coleridge, *Marginalia*, V, 465.

[33] Coleridge, *Marginalia*, V, 413.

[34] Coleridge, *Marginalia*, III, 991.

[35] Coleridge, *Marginalia*, V, 410.

[36] Coleridge, *Marginalia*, V, 406.

[37] Coleridge, *Marginalia*, V, 405, 409, 418.

[38] Coleridge, *Marginalia*, V, 466-7.

[39] Coleridge, *Letters*, IV, 809.

[40] Coleridge, *Marginalia*, III, 992.

Swedenborgian simile in Emersonian edification

A Bicentenary essay 1803-2003

Anders Hallengren

C onsider a scene from an assembly in uproar. In vivid figurative language, the eloquent speaker accuses leading politicians, officials, business-persons, and other upper-class people of highest ranking, of corruption and baseness. Tables are turned. The moment is a period of internal struggle and war. The future of the nation is at stake. Civilisation itself seems to be endangered, and progress is topsy-turvy. Wherever you are, and in whatever direction your thoughts may go, it is easy to recognise the incident as well as the setting. In this particular historical case—Emerson addressing America in Civil War times and during the era of Reconstruction—we will pay special attention to the revolutionary language used by the dismayed orator, who in plain speaking asseverates a home truth.

The upright and the upside-down

In his lecture on American Civilisation, 'Civilization at a Pinch', delivered in Boston in 1861 just after the outbreak of the war, and read again in Washington in January the following year, Emerson opens with a central Swedenborg doctrine: 'Use, labor of each for all, is the health and virtue of all beings'. In this spirit Emerson attacks the 'conspiracy of slavery'...called 'an institution. I call it destitution, this stealing of men and setting them to work, stealing their labor, and the thief sitting idle himself.'[1]

In his address on 'Progress of Culture', read before the Phi Beta Kappa Society at Cambridge in 1867, Emerson emphasises that 'great thoughts come from the heart' and that 'piety is an essential condition of science', mentioning Swedenborg as an example, and a model of both.

Likewise in politics. Challenging the immorality of American public servants, he states:

We have suffered our young men of ambition to play the game of politics and take the immoral side without loss of caste,——to come and go without rebuke. But that kind of loose association does not leave a man his own master. He cannot go from the good to the evil at pleasure, and then back again to the good. There is a text in Swedenborg which tells in figure the plain truth. He saw in vision the angels and the devils; but these two companies stood not face to face and hand in hand, but foot to foot,——these perpendicular up, and those perpendicular down.[2]

This scene illustrates the exact opposite between right and wrong, good and evil.

Swedenborg repeatedly points out that hell is built on earth, and in the next life is the abode of people who feel at home there. In his reports from the intermediary spiritual world, he observes that purposefully choosing evil is like jumping headlong, throwing oneself vertically (*perpendiculariter*) down (*The Spiritual Diary* §2831).

How is this to be understood? A *memorabile* in Swedenborg's book on the Apocalypse, *The Apocalypse Revealed* (§655) is particularly instructive, since it is also repeated in his concluding theological testament, *The True Christian Religion* (§388). There he tells us how faithful people can be like dragons compared to others who believe that love is primary, belief secondary. In a spirited discussion, a representative of the latter clarifies Swedenborg's view. The relation between truth and love is as that between light and its source. If you think you can have light (insight, illumination, truth), which is secondary, before you have the source (neighbourly love, charitas, warmth), which is primary, you will look like someone turned upside-down, with feet up and head down, or like an acrobat who walks on his hands. That is an inverted attitude. Without good works, you cannot get access to the truths of faith.

In the book *Heaven and its Wonders, and Hell* (§§ 510f, 548), another book carefully read by Emerson with pen in his hand, Swedenborg explains how evil souls freely and naturally chose the reversed state since they are bent for the lower. When they throw themselves down into hell from the spiritual world, they appear to fall 'backward headfirst. The reason it looks like this is that such people are in an inverted order' (§ 510).

The art of the genuine

In 'Being and Seeming' (1838), Emerson tells us about an experienced counsellor (Samuel Hoar) who he has heard saying,

> [that he] feared never for the effect upon a jury of a lawyer who does not believe in his heart that his client ought to have a verdict [...] This is that law (is it not?) whereby a work of art, of whatever kind, sets us in the same state of mind as the artist was when he made it. That which we do not believe we cannot adequately say, though we may repeat the words never so often. It was this conviction which Swedenborg expressed when he described a group of persons in the spiritual world endeavoring in vain to articulate a proposition which they did not believe, but they could not, though they twisted and folded their lips even to indignation. But say what you believe and feel, and the voluble air will become music and all surrounding things will dance attendance and coin themselves into words for sense. Every word shall be sovereign, noble, and new, and full of matchless felicities. [...] Truth always overpowers the poor nature of a deceiver [...] Trust *being* and let us seem no longer.[3]

In 'Spiritual Laws', in the first series of *Essays* (1841), Swedenborg's narrative reappears in support of Emerson's belief, that when one 'speaks the truth in the spirit of truth', the eye 'is as clear as the heavens'. The world is 'full of judgement-days', and a man passes for what he is worth. Emerson had arrived at a bright view of man and his world. He is of the opinion that truth is always advantageous, because the world is just. Furthermore, he is certain that everyone can do something better than anyone else. This is the highest benefit of self-trust: to find and fulfil one's object in life. But, as much 'virtue as there is, so much appears; as much goodness as there is, so much reverence it commands'. Man's actual success in his efforts is according to what he is worth: according to the amount of truth and goodness he has in him.

Emerson thus was struck by Swedenborg's memorable relation on the inability of angels to lie, to utter what they do not believe, contained both in *The Apocalypse Revealed* (1766, §294), and in *The True Christian Religion* (1771, §111).[4] He later bought and read the latter work in the translation published in Boston 1847.[5] More important, he secured the former work for his library, in the translation dated Boston 1836, announced in the *New Jerusalem Magazine* in October 1835, and it seems to have occupied him in early 1836.[6] His intense interest can be judged from the fact that a student who was later to become his best-informed critic among New Churchmen, the famous Benjamin Fiske Barrett, was originally introduced by Emerson to Swedenborg: Emerson advised Barrett to check out the *Apocalypse Revealed* from the Harvard College library![7]

The relation found in that book on angels who 'distorted and folded their lips in many ways but could not articulate any other words than such as were consonant with the ideas of their thought', exceedingly attracted Emerson.[8] He quoted it several times. The way he interpreted and used this memorable relation is important: it apparently supported his concepts of the nature of Truth, of Eloquence, of Self-reliance, and of Beauty. It also explains his own imagery. Emerson thought the days of the pilgrims, the days of the founding fathers, were a season of eternal spring, like the Golden Age: 'Massachusetts, in its heroic day, had no government—was an anarchy. Every man stood on his feet'.[9]

Virtue and artistry

In Emerson's outlook there is a strong link between ethics and aesthetics. They are different sides of the same thing. Rightness or accuracy, and the accordance with natural and spiritual laws, is the essence of both.

In his influential 'American Scholar Address' (1837), Emerson called attention to Swedenborg's *literary* value. In this pioneering Cambridge oration, where he put forth a philosophy of life for the New World, he said:

> There is one man of genius who has done much for this philosophy of life, whose literary value has never been rightly estimated;—I mean Emanuel Swedenborg.

The most imaginative of men, yet writing with the precision of a mathematician, he endeavoured to engraft a purely philosophical Ethics on the popular Christianity of his time. Such an attempt of course must have difficulty which no genius could surmount. But he saw and showed the connection between nature and the affections of the soul. He pierced the emblematic or spiritual character of the visible, tangible world. Especially did his shade-loving muse hover over and interpret the lower parts of nature; he showed the mysterious bond that allies moral evil to the foul material forms, and has given in epical parables a theory of insanity, of beasts, of unclean and fearful things. [10]

What is the secret of this power of imagination and the emblematic, then? In 'Poetry and Imagination' (*Letters and Social Aims*, 1875), Emerson explains that the very design of imagination is 'to domesticate us' in 'a celestial nature'. Therefore Emerson praises the symbol as the way of understanding, and time and again stresses its power of clarifying. 'This power is in the image because this power is in Nature. It so affects, because it so is. All that is wondrous in Swedenborg is not his invention, but his extraordinary perception; —that he was necessitated to see', and there are several quotes from Swedenborg in that important aesthetic essay.

Analogously, in his essay on 'Immortality' (*Letters and Social Aims*, 1875) Emerson extols Swedenborg's moral perception, his *second sight,* and the realism of his narratives:

The most remarkable step in the religious history of recent ages is that made by the genius of Swedenborg, who described the moral faculties and affections of man, with the hard realism of an astronomer describing the suns and planets of our system, and explained his opinion of the history and destiny of souls in a narrative form, as of one who had gone in trance into the society of other worlds. Swedenborg described an intelligible heaven, by continuing the like employments in the like circumstances as those we know; men in societies, houses, towns, trades, entertainments; continuations of our earthly experience. We shall pass to the future existence as we enter into an agreeable dream. All nature will accompany us there.[11]

In this spirit Swedenborg appears as both a bard and a law-giver: Emerson, like Coleridge, and Baudelaire, recognised Swedenborg as a great poet. In Emerson's early lecture on 'The Poet', Swedenborg's writings were referred to as 'prose poems'.[12] Still, the 'moral insight of Swedenborg, the correction of popular errors, the announcement of ethical laws, take him out of comparison with any other modern writer and entitle him to a place, vacant for some ages, among the lawgivers of mankind' (*Representative Men*, 1850). What is the connection, then? Emerson at once spells out: 'We have come into a world which is a living poem'.[13] Thus realism and imagination may combine and conflow.

Himself turning to the poetic idiom, Emerson lyrically approaches Swedenborg's significance in the poem 'Solution', published in *May-Day and Other Poems* (1867):

> Far in the North, where polar night
> Holds in check the frolic light,
> In trance upborne past mortal goal
> The Swede EMANUEL leads the soul.
> Through snows above, mines underground,
> The inks of Erebus he found;
> Rehearsed to men the damned wails
> On which the seraph music sails.
> In spirit-worlds he trod alone,
> But walked the earth unmarked, unknown.
> The near bystander caught no sound,——
> Yet they who listened far aloof
> Heard rendings of the skyey roof,
> And felt, beneath, the quaking ground;
> And his air-sown, unheeded words,
> In the next age, are flaming swords.

This is another way of expressing the currency and topicality of the mystic's strange wisdom, which Emerson pointed out in his programmatic 'Editor's Address', printed in *Massachusetts Quarterly Review* in December 1847:

There are literary and philosophical reputations to settle. The name of Swedenborg has in this very time acquired new honors, and the current year has witnessed the appearance, in their first English translation, of his manuscripts. Here is an unsettled account in the book of Fame; a nebula to dim eyes, but which great telescopes may yet resolve into a system.[14]

Here, much remains to be done.

Today, the editor of the present volume assumedly agrees to this point, and, from a scholarly point of view, there are still ample reasons for doing so.

NOTES

[1] R W Emerson, *Miscellanies*, (Boston and New York, 1904), 297. To Emerson, 'use' has always a spiritual and moral meaning. Swedenborg's *Doctrine of Uses* was probably a doctrine that Emerson accepted in full, as I have shown elsewhere: *The Code of Concord* (1994), ch. 'Uses, Utility, and Utilitarianism'; *Gallery of Mirrors* (1998), ch. 'An American Philosophy of Use'.

[2] Emerson, *Letters and Social Aims* (1875) in *The Complete Works of Ralph Waldo Emerson* (W), (Boston and New York 1904), VIII, 233.

[3] Emerson, *Early Lectures* (EL), II, 300f; *Journals and Miscellaneous Notebooks* (JMN), V, 396.

[4] Emerson, JMN, IV, 343. He often returned to this passage.

[5] An indication of earlier cognizance of this work: JMN, V, 7.

[6] Emerson, JMN, V, 115f., 168, 397. The pencil marks in Emerson's copy in the Houghton Library, compared with the earliest excerpts, show that at least the first volume was read before *Nature* (1836) was published.

[7] B F Barrett, *Autobiography*, (Philadelphia, Swedenborg Publishing Association, 1890), 54-55.

[8] E Swedenborg, *Apocalypse Revealed* (1836), I., 254f., §294; 255 marked in Emerson's copy.

[9] Emerson, speech on the Affair in Kansas, W, XI, 261 f.

[10] Emerson, W, I, 112-113.

[11] Emerson, W, VIII, 327.

[12] Emerson, EL, III, 361.

[13] Emerson, W, IV, 115f.

[14] Emerson, *Miscellanies*, 391.

SUPPLEMENT

Books by Emanuel Swedenborg in Emerson's extant Library, now stored in Houghton Library, Harvard, and in the Concord Antiquarian Museum:

The Animal Kingdom, I-II, London 1843-44.

Angelic Wisdom Concerning the Divine Love and the Divine Wisdom, Boston 1847.

The Apocalypse Revealed, I-III, (London 1832), Boston 1836.

The Delights of Wisdom Concerning Conjugal Love, Boston 1843.

The Economy of the Animal Kingdom, London 1845-46.

Heavenly Arcana, I-XII, Boston, 1837-47.

On the Intercourse between the Soul and the Body, which is supposed to take place either by Physical Influx, or by Pre-established Harmony, Boston 1828.

Opuscula, ed. J J G Wilkinson, London 1846.

The Principia, or The First Principles of Natural Things[...], I-II, London and Boston 1845-46.

A Treatise Concerning Heaven and its Wonders, and also Concerning Hell, London 1823.

The True Christian Religion, Boston 1843.

Swedenborgian ideas in the poetry of Elizabeth Barrett Browning and Robert Browning

Richard Lines

Introduction

Browning scholarship has been slow to recognise the influence of Swedenborg's religious philosophy on the work of both poets,[1] although it is well-known that Elizabeth, in particular, was a keen admirer of Swedenborg and during the decade 1850-60 wrote many favourable comments about him in her letters. This has sometimes been seen as an eccentricity on her part, not shared with her husband, and closely connected with her interest in spiritualism during the 1850s. The theme of this paper is that ideas emanating directly or indirectly from Swedenborg's religious writings had a profound impact on the work of the two poets. This should not be considered surprising in the context of the times. Ralph Waldo Emerson visited England in 1847-48 and lectured on Swedenborg, among others. His essay, 'Swedenborg, or the Mystic', was published in *Representative Men* (1850). The Brownings had departed for Italy in September 1846 following their marriage, but their circle of friends in Italy included friends and 'Transcendentalist' associates of Emerson (and fellow readers of Swedenborg), among them Margaret Fuller, who visited the Brownings in Florence immediately before her fateful return to the United States in 1850 (she and her husband were drowned when their ship foundered on rocks off the coast of New Jersey). Contemporary English poets who were also readers of

Swedenborg included Tennyson and Coventry Patmore. The latter's once greatly admired *The Angel in the House* was directly inspired by his reading of *Conjugial Love*.

The Brownings as Readers of Swedenborg

It is not known how and when the Brownings came to be readers of Swedenborg, but there are links with prominent followers of Swedenborg's religious teachings, both in England and later in Italy. Elizabeth Barrett had become acquainted with Charles Augustus Tulk in the 1830s after her favourite uncle had married (as his second wife) the sister of the man already married to Tulk's eldest daughter Caroline. Tulk was a well-known English Swedenborgian and a founder member, and for many years Chairman, of the Swedenborg Society. During the 1830s and early 1840s the widowed Tulk lived at 19 Duke Street, St. James's, while Caroline and her husband lived nearby in the same street. 'We know the Tulks very well, & the Gordons better still', wrote Elizabeth to her friend Mary Russell Mitford on 27 October 1842.[2] At this time Elizabeth does not seem to have been particularly impressed by Tulk (or by Swedenborg's writings). He was, she wrote to her friend, 'a clever man...but probably of no great depth—which I don't in the least say on account of Mesmer,—no, nor even of Swedenborg—but these universal men *can't* be deep—it is out of the nature of things.'[3] These remarks sound a little dismissive about a man who at this time had some standing in public life (he had sat twice as a Member of Parliament, was an active magistrate in Middlesex and, from 1839 to 1847, Chairman of the committee of management of the famous Hanwell Pauper Lunatic Asylum) and had corresponded with Samuel Taylor Coleridge on terms of intellectual equality.

It was not, apparently, until some years later that Tulk introduced Elizabeth (and her husband) to one work in particular of Swedenborg's, viz. *Conjugial Love*. Elizabeth Barrett had married Robert Browning in London in September 1846 and, after spending their first winter together in Pisa, they had settled in Florence in the spring of 1847. In September 1847 Tulk's youngest child Sophia married Henry Cottrell, court chamberlain to the Duke of Lucca, who had given him the honorary title of Count. Tulk joined them in Florence in early 1848. He visited the Brownings regularly, often coming on his own. 'He lends us Swedenborg & Blake's poems', Elizabeth told her sister Henrietta in a letter (21 February—4 March 1848).[4] She went on to tell her sister, [that he] has lent us a book on *Conjugal* [sic] *Love*, which is a marriage gift to his own children, & Robert and I are reading it devoutly…though I do assure you Henrietta, it contains some very extrordinary-sounding paragraphs, which Robert makes a point of reading aloud just because I don't like it. After we have done, we hide the book in the shadiest corner of the room, lest somebody, not quite as spiritual as a Swedenborgian, might make the wrong deductions from it: but there are some beautiful things really, & the angels who float up & down the pages in blue tunics, are refreshing to look upon.

Both the Brownings warmed to Tulk, 'Yes, he is perfectly good,' Elizabeth wrote to Henrietta, 'Robert said the other day, "he felt quite *attached* to him". He seems to live in the light of God's & man's love—& Swedenborgian or not, he is Christian in the largest sense' (22 April 1848).[5] It appears that Tulk was in poor health at the time (he was to die in January 1849, shortly after his return to England) and told Elizabeth that now his daughters were happily married 'he would gladly retreat into the new world' (letter to her sister Arabella 10-11 May 1847).[6] In the same letter she reported verbatim Tulk's words to her:

"Tell me," he asked, "…if Mr Browning were to go from you, wouldn't you desire to rejoin him?—I want to go to my wife—There's no other tie in life like that tie. What exists between a parent & child, is comparatively nothing—merely temporal— Conjugal [*sic*] love is the one eternal bond which God has set his seal on."

Susanna Tulk had died in 1824. Charles never remarried, believing that their love was truly 'conjugial' in the Swedenborgian sense and that they would be reunited in the next world. This is exactly the view that both Brownings came to express in their poetry, as will be shown. It is also apparent from the same letter that Robert and Tulk's eldest son, Augustus Henry, had been acquainted when they were both students at the fledgling University of London (later University College London) in 1828-9.

Robert Browning had made the acquaintance of another Swedenborgian, the physician

James John Garth Wilkinson (who knew Tulk), in the late 1830s. They were exact contemporaries. Wilkinson had attended a private reading of Browning's play *Strafford* and was at Covent Garden for the first performance on 1 May 1837.[7] It appears that Wilkinson encouraged Robert to read Swedenborg. In old age Browning recalled these early days in a letter to Wilkinson thanking him for the gift of a book:

> I well remember the letter in which you recommended me to study Swedenborg. I believe that you and I have always been in accordance as to aspiration and sympathy, though we may differ in our appreciation of facts connected with them.[8]

It is not known which of Swedenborg's works Robert Browning read on Wilkinson's recommendation, but there are over 120 references to Swedenborg in the Brownings' correspondence, 64 references to Swedenborgianism or Swedenborgians and one reference each to *Arcana Caelestia, Apocalypse Explained* and *Heaven and Hell*.[9] Elizabeth's commonplace book contains passages from *Divine Love and Wisdom* and *Divine Providence* on topics which include the Incarnation, regeneration, the Trinity and hereditary evil.[10]

Soon after their arrival in Florence the Brownings became friends with yet another follower of Swedenborg's religious teachings, the American sculptor Hiram Powers. Born in Vermont in 1805, but brought up in Cincinnati, Ohio, Powers had first formed an enthusiasm for Swedenborg's religious writings as a young man. He and his wife moved to Florence in 1837 and he was to live there until his death in 1873. The Brownings met him soon after their arrival in Florence in the spring of 1847 and it was in his studio in the Via dei Senagli (a short distance from Casa Guidi) in May that year that Elizabeth first saw his celebrated sculpture 'The Greek Slave' (which was later to delight visitors to the Great Exhibition in Hyde Park in 1851). Elizabeth was inspired to write her sonnet, 'Hiram Powers' "Greek Slave" ', which was published in her 1850 volume of poems. Powers was baptised into the Swedenborgian or New Church in 1850 by the Rev Thomas Worcester, a well-known American Swedenborgian clergyman, who may be the 'Swedenborg priest' referred to in recently discovered (but unpublished) correspondence between Powers and Elizabeth.[11] A letter from Powers to Elizabeth dated 7 August 1853 expounds Swedenborg's doctrine of the spiritual body and also associates the whiteness of ancient Greek statues (apparently Winckelmann thought they were white) with Plato's theory of ideal forms.[12] Powers was probably also influenced in these ideas by J Flaxman (incidentally, another Swedenborgian and a close friend of Tulk), a copy of whose *Lectures on Sculpture* he owned.

Another American Swedenborgian whom the Brownings knew in Florence was the painter William Page, sometimes known as 'the American Titian'. He had met Powers in Florence and soon became an ardent Swedenborgian. Although he had come to Florence in 1850, he did not meet the Brownings until the winter of 1853-4. By early January 1854 Elizabeth was calling Page an 'immense favourite' and Robert wrote to John Forster in London that he had never seen such brilliant contemporary art as that of Page.[13] Page (and his troubled marriage) are depicted by Robert Browning in his poem 'Andrea del Sarto', which contains some interesting (and probably Swedenborgian) references to the dimensions of the holy city, the New Jerusalem.[14]

In 1853 Elizabeth wrote to her friend Isa Blagden (who had also been reading Swedenborg):

> I have not read the *Arcana* and some other of his works, and, of what I have read, the *Heaven and Hell* struck me most. He is wonderful, it seems to me—his scheme of the natural and spiritual worlds and natures appears to me, in an internal light of its own, divine and true...I receive it as a self-evident verity of which one wonders "Why did I not think of that before?"...he is the only thinker who throws any light on the so-called manifestations which are increasing on all sides of us.[15]

The reference to 'manifestations' is to the 'craze' for spiritualism that swept North America and Europe following reports of the 'rapping' experiences of the Fox sisters in New York State in 1848. By 1850 the two young girls (by then aged thirteen and eleven) were giving demonstrations in New York City at $100 a night.[16] The 'craze' had reached Europe by 1852 and there is no doubt that Elizabeth took a great interest in the subject and certainly believed that communication with spirits of the departed was possible. While her husband remained sceptical, her enthusiasm was shared by others, including convinced Swedenborgians like Hiram Powers. On a visit to England in the summer of 1855 the Brownings attended a séance—given by the well-known American medium, the Scottish-born Daniel Dunglas

Home, at the Ealing home of the solicitor John Snaith Rymer—at which Elizabeth was crowned with a wreath of clematis by a 'spirit hand'.[17] Robert was disgusted by the episode and thought that the young American had worked on the susceptibilities of his wife. After her death he satirised Home in 'Mr Sludge the Medium', although, as G K Chesterton pointed out,[18] the poem is in a sense a defence of Sludge. While Robert did not believe in intercourse with spirits, he certainly did believe (and particularly after Elizabeth's death) in a conscious life beyond this one. There is a specific reference to Swedenborg in the poem, his name being coupled with that of St Paul.

Love and Marriage in this World and the Next

The influence of Swedenborg's religious writings (and *Conjugial Love* in particular) on the poetry of the Brownings may, I believe, be seen most clearly in their treatment of the spiritual nature of marriage. In *Conjugial Love* Swedenborg depicted true marriage love between man and woman as a perfect mirroring of the divine. The theme of marriage love runs like a *leitmotiv* through the poems of both Robert and Elizabeth. Towards the end of her great 'novel in verse', *Aurora Leigh* (published in 1857), the hero Romney Leigh tells his cousin, the poet Aurora, that the 'love of wedded souls' stands second only to God's love:

> Which still presents that mystery's counterpart.
> Sweet shadow-rose, upon the water of life,
> Of such a mystic substance, Sharon gave
> A name to! human, vital, fructuous rose,
> Whose calyx holds the multitude of leaves,
> Loves filial, loves fraternal, neighbour-loves
> And civic – all fair petals, all good scents,
> All reddened, sweetened from one central Heart![19]

As Professor Kerry McSweeney points out in his introduction to the 1993 Oxford edition of the poem (page xxxiv), only Coventry Patmore's *The Angel in the House* comes close to matching 'the exalted status and divine aura with which marriage is invested in *Aurora Leigh*', although he does not mention the common source of inspiration for both poems.

McSweeney quotes a contemporary Roman Catholic reviewer of *Aurora Leigh* who described wedded love as 'the key-note of Mrs Browning's poem' which is 'proclaimed to be the essence of Christianity' and the 'centre and *summum bonum* of humanity'.[20]

In her *Sonnets from the Portuguese*, forty-four exquisite sonnets in which she expresses her love for Robert, Elizabeth alludes to a love that will survive the death of the physical body. Sonnet XLIII, the best-known of all, which begins with the line, 'How do I love thee? Let me count the ways', ends with the poet expressing her faith that their love will survive death:

> I love thee with a love I seemed to lose
> With my lost saints,——I love thee with the breath,
> Smiles, tears, of all my life!——and, if God choose,
> I shall but love thee better after death.

Towards the end of her life Elizabeth supposed that after she died Robert, as a man, would be capable of some 'feeble bigamy'. For her (and, it turned out, for Robert also), true marriage (as Swedenborg had taught in *Conjugial Love*) was for eternity, not just for this earthly life. Some years after Elizabeth's death Robert contemplated marriage with Lady Ashburton, a beautiful and wealthy widow, but things went no further after he had told her that the marriage would be for the sake of his son and that he had buried his heart in Florence.[21] In 'Any Wife to any Husband', published during Elizabeth's lifetime in the 1855 volume *Men and Women*, Robert wrote of a dying wife who implores her husband to remain faithful to her memory after her death:

> Because thou once hast loved me——wilt thou dare
> Say to thy soul and Who may list beside,
> 'Therefore she is immortally my bride;
> Chance cannot change my love, nor time impair.'
>
> (IX)

She knows that, as a man, her husband will yearn for 'the fresher faces', but, even if he does give his love elsewhere, he will return to her in spirit:

> Re-coin thyself and give it them to spend,——
> It all comes to the same thing in the end,
> Since mine thou wast, mine art and mine shalt be,
> Faithful or faithless, sealing up the sum
> Or lavish of my treasure, thou must come
> Back to the heart's place here I keep for thee!

(XVI)

In Elizabeth's Bible after her death in 1861 Robert inscribed some words from Dante's *La Vita Nuova*: 'I believe and I declare——Certain am I——from this life I pass into a better, there where that lady lives of whom enamoured was my soul'.[22] He was later to incorporate these words into his poem 'La Saisiaz', musings on the subject of immortality written in the aftermath of the sudden death of his friend Anne Egerton Smith while she, Robert and his sister Sarianna were on holiday together in French Savoy in September 1877.

In 'The Last Ride Together' (also from *Men and Women*) he writes of a ride taken by lovers who are about to part for ever. In the last stanza the man expresses his hope that they will meet again in heaven:

> What if we still ride on, we two
> With life for ever old yet new,
> Changed not in kind but in degree,
> The instant made eternity,——
> And heaven just prove that I and she
> Ride, ride together, for ever ride?

(X)

In 'Evelyn Hope', a poem from the same volume and much loved by the Victorians, a middle aged man longs for union in the next world with a girl who had died at sixteen, too young for love in this world:

But the time will come,——at last it will,

When, Evelyn Hope, what meant (I shall say)

In the lower earth, in the years long still,

That body and soul so pure and gay?

Why your hair was amber, I shall divine,

And your mouth of your own geranium's red——

And what you would do with me, in fine,

In the new life come in the old one's stead.

(V)

The philosophy behind the poem is certainly consonant with the teaching of Swedenborg that those who do not find true marriage love in this world may find it in the next. Browning may even have heard from Tulk or Wilkinson the anecdote that Swedenborg had told friends during his lifetime that the Countess Gyllenborg would be his wife in the spiritual world.[23]

Christians have sometimes found difficulty with Swedenborg's concept of married angels because it seems to conflict with Luke 20:35 that in heaven there is neither marriage nor giving in marriage. Dr John Chadwick, the most recent translator into English of *Conjugial Love*, thought that the original Greek words refer to weddings, not to the continuing state of matrimony.[24] Robert Browning, a considerable Greek scholar as well as a reader of *Conjugial Love*, seems to have taken a similar view. At the end of 'Pompilia', Book VII of his immense poem *The Ring and the Book*, the dying heroine looks forward to union in the next world with her lover and father of her baby son, the Roman Catholic priest Caponsacchi, in these words:

Marriage on earth seems such a counterfeit,

Mere imitation of the inimitable:

In heaven we have the real and true and sure.

'Tis there they neither marry nor are given

In marriage but are as the angels: right,

Oh how right that is, how like Jesus Christ

———

To say that! Marriage-making for the earth,

With gold so much,——birth, power, repute so much,

Or beauty, youth so much, in lack of these!

Be as the angels rather, who, apart,

Know themselves into one, are found at length

Married, but marry never, no, nor give

In marriage; they are man and wife at once

When the true time is...[25]

At the end of Book I of *The Ring and the Book* Browning apostrophises his dead wife, addressing her as his 'lyric Love, half-angel and half-bird' and yearns for communion with her:

That still, despite the distance and the dark,

What was, again may be; some interchange

Of grace, some splendour once thy very thought,

Some benediction anciently thy smile...[26]

In an earlier poem, 'Prospice', in the volume *Dramatis Personae* published in 1864, Browning makes a clear reference to his belief that he will meet Elizabeth again when he dies:

And the elements' rage, the fiend-voices that rave,

Shall dwindle, shall blend,

Shall change, shall become first a peace out of pain,

Then a light, then thy breast,

O thou soul of my soul! I shall clasp thee again,

And with God be the rest!

(lines 23-28)

God is known in Jesus Christ the Divine Human

Central to Swedenborg's theology is the teaching that God is one, manifested to us as the Divine Human, the Lord Jesus Christ. Swedenborg believed in the doctrine of the Trinity,

—

regarding Father, Son and Holy Ghost as the three essentials of the one God. This teaching is clearly reflected in the poetry of both Brownings. In *The True Christian Religion* §135.4, Swedenborg explains that God the Father, the infinite being or *esse*, cannot be approached by man because he would be destroyed, as wood is destroyed by fire. In 'Bishop Blougram's Apology' Robert Browning writes:

> Naked belief in God the Omnipotent,
> Omniscient, Omnipresent, sears too much
> The sense of conscious creatures to be borne,
> It were the seeing him, no flesh shall dare.
>
> . . . .
>
> Under a vertical sun, the exposed brain
> And lidless eye and disemprisoned heart
> Less certainly would wither up at once,
> Than mind, confronted with the truth of him.
>
> (lines 620-623 and 630-633)

God can only be understood and approached as a man, teaches Swedenborg. Robert Browning, too, can only worship a man:

> Whom have I in mind
> Thus worshipping, unless a man, my like,
> Howe'er above me? *Man*, I say——how else,
> I being man how worship?
>
> 'The Sun' (lines 49-52)
> *Ferishtah's Fancies* (1884)

In *Aurora Leigh* (Book VIII, lines 558-561) Elizabeth uses a specific Swedenborgian expression, 'Divine Humanity', and echoes Swedenborg in *Arcana Caelestia* (§1940), where he writes that the 'internal' is the 'inmost' part of man and is what distinguishes him from animals and provides the door or entrance for God:

———

> But innermost
> Of the inmost, most interior of the interne,
> God claims His own, Divine humanity
> Renewing nature——...

Robert makes it plain that Christ is God. In the remarkable poem 'Karshish' (in *Men and Women*) a sceptical Syrian physician visits Jerusalem to investigate the story of a man Lazarus, still living, who was said to have been raised from the dead by Jesus of Nazareth many years before. Karshish relates (in the form of a letter to a friend) how :

> This man so cured regards the curer, then,
> As——God forgive me! who but God himself,
> Creator and sustainer of the world,
> That came and dwelt in flesh on it awhile!
>
> ....
>
> The very God! think, Abib: dost thou think?
> So, the All-Great, were the All-Loving too—
> So, through the thunder comes a human voice
> Saying, 'O heart I made, a heart beats here!...'
>
> (lines 268-271 and 305-308)

In his great poem, 'A Death in the Desert', about the death and dying utterances of John the Evangelist and author of the Book of Revelation (in the poem they are assumed to be the same person, but that was a matter of great controversy in Browning's day) Browning ends with very strong statements of Christ's divinity. The narrator (an old man who had known John) describes how John 'Lies as he lay once [at the Last Supper], breast to breast with God' and declares:

> Call Christ, then, the ILLIMITABLE GOD,
> Or lost!

Correspondences

Swedenborg's doctrine that everything in our natural world 'corresponds' with something in a higher spiritual reality is given powerful voice in *Aurora Leigh*:

> There's not a flower of spring
> That dies ere June, but vaunts itself allied,
> By issue and symbol, by significance
> And correspondence, to that spirit-world
> Outside the limits of our space and time,
> Whereto we are bound.

(Book V, lines 120-125)

That our world is the 'effect' of a spiritual 'cause' as taught by Swedenborg is also illustrated in this poem:

> And verily many thinkers of this age,
> Aye, many Christian teachers, half in heaven,
> Are wrong in just my sense, who understood
> Our natural world too insularly, as if
> No spiritual counterpart completed it
> Consummating its meaning, rounding all
> To justice and perfection, line by line,
> Form by form, nothing single or alone,
> The great below clenched by the great above,
> Shade here authenticating substance there,
> The body proving spirit, as the effect
> The cause:

(Book VIII, lines 614-625)

Elsewhere in *Aurora Leigh* Elizabeth illustrates, in relation to poetic inspiration, Swedenborg's teaching that there is an inflowing from the spiritual to the natural, not the other way round:

> What form is best for poems? Let me think
> Of forms less, and the external. Trust the spirit,
> As sovran nature does, to make the form;
> For otherwise we only imprison spirit
> And not embody. Inward evermore
> To outward—so in life, and so in art
> Which still is life.

(Book V, lines 223-229)

Other Teachings from Swedenborg

Illustrations can be found in Robert Browning's poetry of other Swedenborgian teachings. Swedenborg explains in *Arcana Caelestia* (§ 7290) that miracles do not occur in the present day because they would compel belief. Browning echoes this in some lines from 'A Death in the Desert':

> I say, that miracle was duly wrought,
> When, save for it, no faith was possible.
>
> . . . .
>
> So faith grew, making void more miracles
> Because too much: they would compel, not help.

(lines 461-462 and 469-470)

In 'Bishop Blougram's Apology' he expounds Swedenborg's teaching that man is held in an 'equilibrium' between good and evil. In no other way would spiritual growth be possible:

> No, when the fight begins within himself,
> A man's worth something. God stoops o'er his head,
> Satan looks up between his feet—both tug—
> He's left, himself, i' the middle: the soul wakes
> And grows. Prolong that battle through his life!

Never leave growing till the life to come!

(lines 665-670)

Throughout his poetry Robert Browning emphasises the importance of living life to the full. Only then can the soul develop. He warns against the 'unlit lamp' and the 'ungirt loin' ('The Statue and the Bust') and the notion that 'heaven repairs what wrong earth's journey did' ('Bifurcation'). This seems very much in accord with Swedenborg's teaching that our 'ruling love' (derived from how we have lived in this world) will determine our eternal destiny:

> Fool! All that is, at all,
> Lasts ever, past recall;
> Earth changes, but thy soul and God stand sure:
> What entered into thee,
> *That* was, is, and shall be:
> Time's wheel runs back or stops: Potter and clay endure.
>
> ('Rabbi Ben Ezra', XXVII)

For him, as for Swedenborg, hell is self-chosen and never willed by God for anyone. The traditional doctrine of a burning hell was still very much alive in the middle of the nineteenth century, but Browning affirms Swedenborg's remarkable doctrine that every spirit, whether good or bad, is permitted to be in its own delight:

> Let the unjust usurp at will:
> The filthy shall be filthy still:
> Miser, there awaits the gold for thee!
> Hater, indulge thine enmity!
> And thou, whose heaven self-ordained
> Was, to enjoy earth unrestrained,
> Do it!...
>
> ('Easter-Day' XXII, cf. Revelation 22:11)

37

For Robert Browning, there could be no God without love and here, too, he is close to the heart of Swedenborg's teaching that God is love itself:

> For the loving worm within its clod,
> Were diviner than a loveless God
> Amid his worlds, I will dare to say.
>
> ('Christmas-Eve' V)

For Elizabeth also, love is supreme because it is identified with God:

> Art is much, but love is more.
> O Art, my Art, thou'rt much, but Love is more!
> Art symbolises heaven, but Love is God
> And makes heaven.
>
> (*Aurora Leigh*, Book IX, lines 656-659)

The New Jerusalem

One of Swedenborg's most important teachings concerns the interpretation of John's vision of the holy city, the New Jerusalem, in Chapter 21 of the Book of Revelation. In the introduction to his short work *The New Jerusalem*[27] Swedenborg tells the reader that the New Jerusalem is not a city, but (in effect) a new age of spiritual truth and enlightenment for mankind. Elizabeth Barrett Browning ends *Aurora Leigh* with a magnificent evocation of this:

> The world's old,
> But the old world waits the time to be renewed,
> Toward which, new hearts in individual growth
> Must quicken, and increase to multitude
> In new dynasties of the race of men;
> Developed whence, shall grow spontaneously
> New churches, new economies, new laws

> Admitting freedom, new societies
> Excluding falsehood: HE shall make all things new.
>
> (Book IX, lines 941-949)

Robert Browning also draws from the end of the Book of Revelation at the conclusion of his somewhat gnomic poem, 'Epilogue to Dramatis Personae', the last in the volume *Dramatis Personae* (1864), the first book he published after Elizabeth's death. There are three speakers in the poem. The first is the biblical King David, who tells of the thousands who filled the Lord's temple. The second speaker is Browning's contemporary the French writer Ernest Renan, whose *Life of Jesus* (1863) treated him simply as an historical figure. This section is about loss of faith. The third speaker (not named) appears to be the poet himself. He reaffirms his faith for the contemporary age by re-stating it as a personal faith in Jesus Christ without the trappings of organised religion:

> Why, where's the need of Temple, when the walls
> O' the world are that? What use of swells and falls
> From Levites' choir, Priests' cries, and trumpet-calls?
>
> That one Face, far from vanish, rather grows,
> Or decomposes but to recompose,
> Become my universe that feels and knows.
>
> (XI and XII)

The Browning of this poem puzzled contemporary critics. One reviewer thought that he more resembled the American writers Emerson, Wendell Holmes and Bigelow than any English poet of the time.[28] Another (slightly later) critic, Edward Dowden, called Browning 'The Militant Transcendentalist' and felt he had made away with the historical Jesus of Nazareth, dissolving him into a 'Christ-myth'.[29]

Conclusion

It was accepted among Swedenborgians of the late nineteenth and early twentieth centuries that the poetry of both the Brownings had been influenced by Swedenborg.[30] That influence does not seem to have been noted in wider literary and religious circles, although Robert Browning in particular was long regarded (and much quoted) as a major religious poet. In a remarkable study of his poetry [31] Dallas Kenmare says that, 'There is, indeed, no other great English poet so consistently and constantly Christian as Browning'. She goes on to say that he is never classed as a devotional poet like Henry Vaughan, George Herbert, Alice Meynell or Francis Thompson because 'A liberal breadth of outlook, a grandeur, freedom and sanity, in short, a "wholeness" in Browning's personality will always exclude him from any narrow categories or classifications'. She describes his position as 'essentially unorthodox' (192), although he was certainly a 'liberal Christian'. 'He recognises elements of truth in every sect, but absolute and final truth in none, because, in all, truth is falsified, even if only slightly, by man-imposed doctrine, and in this life, knowledge of truth can never be more than partial' (192). Swedenborg himself, who never sought to establish a religious sect called 'the New Church', emphasises in a number of passages[32] that no Christian denomination has a monopoly of truth, although all have truth within them.

In Florence the Brownings had close friends like Hiram Powers and William Page who were members of the small New Church community in the city, but neither of them ever sought to join that congregation. Both poets had been brought up as dissenters, but they had married according to the rites and ceremonies of the Church of England. Their son Pen was baptised in the French Protestant Church in Florence.[33] Poets of genius cannot always be confined within the tenets of any religious sect and that was certainly the case with the Brownings. They needed no clerical intermediaries, but drew from a wide range of reading and study, including Swedenborg.[34]

To argue that ideas derived from Swedenborg's religious writings helped to inspire the two poets is not to attempt to detract from the achievement of either Elizabeth or Robert Browning, but, hopefully, readers will be assisted to reach a deeper understanding of the ideas embodied in their poetry of love and religion. Likewise, it is to be hoped that some may be moved to explore the work of a thinker and seer who has for far too long been either neglected or marginalised in Western culture.

NOTES

[1] One recent biographical study does, however, mention the probable influence on both Brownings of Swedenborg's *Conjugial Love* (in the original Latin of this work, Swedenborg's spelling of the adjective is *conjugialis*, not the more usual *conjugalis*): Julia Markus, *Dared and Done: the Marriage of Elizabeth Barrett and Robert Browning*, (London, Bloomsbury, 1995), 219, 282.

[2] *The Brownings' Correspondence*, ed. Philip Kelley, Ronald Hudson, and Scott Lewis, (Winfield, KS, Wedgestone Press, 1984-), 6, 124.

[3] *The Brownings' Correspondence*, 6, 127 – 128.

[4] Scott Lewis, 'Sophia Cottrell's Recollections' in *Browning Society Notes*, Vol. 24 (1997), 17,18. A transcript of this letter is in Dr Lewis's possession.

[5] Lewis,18. A transcript of the letter is in Dr Lewis's possession.

[6] Lewis,19. MS: The Henry W & Albert A Berg Collection, the New York Public Library, Astor, Lenox and Tilden Foundations.

[7] C J Wilkinson, *James John Garth Wilkinson*, (London, Kegan Paul, Trench, Trübner, 1911), 31-32.

[8] Wilkinson, 206. The letter is dated 17 May 1887.

[9] Letter from Dr Philip Kelley to the author. Elizabeth made two pages of notes on *Apocalypse Explained* in French. These are at Yale.

[10] Robert W Gladish, 'Elizabeth Barrett Browning and Swedenborg', *New Church Life*, (Bryn Athyn, PA, 1965), 559, 567. Elizabeth's notebook is in the Huntington Library, San Marino, California. The quotation from *Divine Love and Wisdom* is in Latin, while the passages from *Divine Providence* appear to be her own translations into English.

[11] Gladish, 560. The information about the recently discovered correspondence was kindly given to the author by Katerina Gaja.

[12] Information about this letter was supplied to the author by Katerina Gaja.

[13] Gladish, 564.

[14] Markus, 199.

[15] Edward C McAleer, *New Letters from Mrs Browning to Isa Blagden*, PMLA, LXVI (September 1951), 596.

[16] Gladish, 508.

[17] Markus, 229-232. Home (1833-1886) had also given a séance at the home of Dr Garth Wilkinson that summer. Wilkinson was sufficiently impressed to write a detailed account of Home's performance for the *Morning Advertiser*. His brother, William Wilkinson, a solicitor and former Secretary of the Swedenborg Society, actually wrote the bulk of Home's memoirs, *Incidents in my Life* (1863), from information supplied by Home and wrote the preface to the second edition published the following year: *Dictionary of National Biography*, Vol. IX, (London, 1908), 1119.

[18] G K Chesterton, *Robert Browning*, (London, Macmillan, 1903, 1930), 51-52. Chesterton

says that Browning was 'a kind of cosmic detective who walked into the foulest of thieves' kitchens and accused men publicly of virtue'.

[19] Elizabeth Barrett Browning, *Aurora Leigh*, ed. with introduction by Kerry McSweeney, (Oxford, OUP, 1993), Book IX, lines 883-890.

[20] *Richard Simpson as Critic*, ed. David Carroll, (London, 1977), 79. For the influence of Swedenborg on the poetry of Coventry Patmore see J C Reid, *The Mind and Art of Coventry Patmore,* (London, Routledge Kegan Paul, 1957).

[21] Markus, 282.

[22] Markus, 282.

[23] Wilkinson, 234 and C O Sigstedt, *The Swedenborg Epic*, (London, The Swedenborg Society, 1981), 464. Elaine Baly, a descendant of one of Browning's uncles, believes that 'Evelyn Hope' was written for Charles Dickens. Dickens was grievously affected by the death in 1837 of his sister-in-law Mary Hogarth at the age of seventeen: information given to the author by Elaine Baly. See also Peter Ackroyd, *Dickens*, (London, Sinclair Stevenson, 1990), 225-229, where Dickens' extraordinary grief over Mary's death is described.

[24] Translator's introduction to *Conjugial Love*, (London, The Swedenborg Society, 1996), x.

[25] *The Ring and the Book*, ed. Richard Altick, (Harmondsworth, Penguin, 1971, 1990), Book VII, lines 1824-1837.

[26] *The Ring and the Book*, Book I, lines 1406-1409. Much later in the work, in Book X, 'The Pope', there appears to be a specific reference to Swedenborg as 'the sagacious Swede' (line 292). Altick says that he is 'unidentified', but C W Hodell, in his notes to the Everyman edition of 1911, says that this 'evidently' refers to Swedenborg, although the reference is an anachronistic one. Browning based his poem on a real murder case dating from 1698 and the Pope is Pope Innocent XII.

[27] *introducing the New Jerusalem*, (London, The Swedenborg Society, 2003), 110. The translation is by John Chadwick.

[28] William Stigand in *The Edinburgh Review*, October 1864, cxx, 537-565, anthologised in *Browning: the Critical Heritage*, ed. Boyd Litzinger and Donald Smalley, (London, Routledge Kegan Paul, 1970), 230. The three American writers were all readers of Swedenborg. John Bigelow, who died in 1911 at the age of 94, was for a time joint proprietor and editor with William Cullen Bryant of the New York *Evening Post* and at the end of his life a Vice-President (along with Henry James) of the International Swedenborg Congress held in London in 1910 to celebrate the centenary of the Swedenborg Society.

[29] Edward Dowden, 'The Transcendental Movement in Literature', in *Contemporary Review,* (July 1877), xxx. 297-318: Litzinger and Smalley, 427. Dowden later wrote a biography of Browning which was published in 1904.

[30] In his concluding remarks at the International Swedenborg Congress the President, Edward Broadfield, said that, 'Robert and Elizabeth Browning have given us literature directly influenced

by Swedenborg': *Transactions of the International Swedenborg Congress*, (London, The Swedenborg Society, 1912), 330. Broadfield and other Swedenborgians were probably influenced by an essay by James Spilling, *Swedenborg and the Brownings*, (London, James Speirs, 1886), from which some of my examples have been taken. Spilling (1825-97) was editor of the *Eastern Daily Press* and a novelist. See also 'Robert Browning's Relation to New Church Theology' by the same author in *New Church Magazine* (1887), 10.

[31] Dallas Kenmare, *An End to Darkness: a New Approach to Robert Browning and His Work*, (London, Peter Owen, 1962), 191.

[32] Examples include *Divine Providence* (§259), where Swedenborg states that if all Christians possessed charity and faith their intellectual dissensions would not have divided the church, but would only have varied it, as light varies colours in beautiful objects.

[33] Clyde de Ryals, *The Life of Robert Browning: A Critical Biography*, (Oxford, Blackwell, 1993), 94.

[34] A possible 'clerical intermediary' is Frederick Denison Maurice, the 'Broad Church' Anglican theologian and 'Christian Socialist', whose views were widely influential at the time. Maurice (1805-1872) was dismissed from his professorship at King's College, London for his liberal views. In *Aurora Leigh* Romney is described as a 'Christian Socialist': Book V, line 737. Maurice was also a reader of Swedenborg: William Raeper, *George MacDonald*, (Tring, Lion, 1987), 240. The annual report of the Swedenborg Society for the year 1859-1860, commenting on the spread of 'Broad Church' ideas in the Church of England as 'the natural outflow of New Church truths', stated that it was no regret if people would rather take these truths from Maurice and Kingsley than 'from the fountainhead', i.e. Swedenborg. William Wilkinson was Secretary of the Society at that time.

A Hermeneutic Key to the title *Leaves of Grass*

Anders Hallengren

In his international bestseller *The Western Canon: The Books and School of the Ages* (first ed. 1994), Harold Bloom stresses the central position of Walt Whitman (1819-1892) in American literature, and in Western poetry in general. In a chapter entitled 'Walt Whitman as center of the American Canon', the American professor overviews American contributions to art and culture. He does so in a mood of despondency:

> If one attempts to list the artistic achievements of our nation against the background of Western tradition, our accomplishments in music, painting, sculpture, architecture tend to be somewhat dwarfed. It is no question of using Bach, Mozart, and Beethoven as the standard; Stravinsky, Schoenberg, and Bartók are more than enough to place our composers in a somewhat sad perspective. And whatever the splendors of modern American painting and sculpture, there has been no Matisse among us. The Walt Whitman as Center of the American Canon exception is in literature. [1]

Whitman was to influence future generations of poets, in the USA as well as in Europe. He

---

had no direct contemporary predecessors, but for a poet-philosopher: Ralph Waldo Emerson. Harold Bloom time and again returns to the importance of Emerson to Whitman.[2] Through the years, many prominent Whitman scholars have done so, too. Bringing the matter to a head, Newton Arvin observed that Emerson was as important to Whitman as Epicurus to Lucretius or Spinoza to Goethe.[3]

However momentous and monumental, prophetic, modern or timeless Whitman's work may be regarded in retrospect, things looked different in his own time. When *Leaves of Grass* was set, printed and published by the author himself in 1855, all at his own cost, that classic was as much a failure as Henry David Thoreau's *Walden* (1854), and Herman Melville's *Moby Dick* (1851) had been. At least momentarily. There were not many people reading such odd and non-conformist literature. Their recognition came later, and was eventually to propel all three into worldwide fame.

Whitman's completely unconventional prose poems, written in a style not seen since Middle Age folk literature or Old Testament songs and verses and texts of most ancient date—and furthermore marked by a positive sensuality and undogmatic (yet far from ungodly) world-embracing piety and love—seemed as insignificant as depraved, and certainly ill-timed.

There were indeed some striking responses. One of his readers is said to have thrown his copy into the fire—the natural way of disposing of things in those days. However, there were a few favourable reactions, too, and Whitman carefully collected them as precious gems, as almost any author would have done. When he found a publisher for his book in 1856, he quoted them in print. First of all a letter from the (in)famous Emerson, who also had one of his early publications burnt and destroyed—the printed version of his similarly devout and unchurchly 'Divinity School Address' (1838); an edition that disappeared completely and forever.

Emerson saluted Whitman's collection of poems as 'the most extraordinary piece of wit and wisdom that an American has yet contributed' [!] and greeted the young writer 'at the beginning of a great career'. Whitman quoted that letter in the second edition (1856) where he also paid tribute to Emerson, his 'Master'. Whitman's indebtedness was explicit, and the poet from Long Island seems to have been touched by the influential Concord mind already in the 1840s. In his letter, Emerson also added that *Leaves of*

Grass must have a long background somewhere. Presumably he realised that he belonged to that background himself.[4]

Second, and of special interest, Whitman found that his book of poetry had been enthusiastically received by some people in his own New York neighbourhood. That review was published in *The Christian Spiritualist*, a journal founded by a group of Swedenborgians. *Leaves of Grass* was reviewed as a great work which partly embodied and realised the wisdom of Swedenborg's doctrines. That critique was accordingly quoted, and obviously appreciated by Whitman himself, in 'Leaves-Droppings', in *Leaves of Grass,* (Brooklyn, New York 1856), 363ff. It read:

> rare is it to find any receiver of 'the heavenly doctrines' determined to enter for himself into the very interiors of all that Swedenborg taught——to see, not the mighty reflections that Swedenborg was able to give of interior realities, but their originals, as they stand constellated in the heavens! [...] Ralph Waldo Emerson is the highest type. He sees the future of truths as our Spirit-seers discern the future of man. [*Leaves of Grass* is] written, as we perceive, under powerful influxes; a prophecy and promise of much that awaits all who are entering with us into the opening doors of a new Era.[5]

In this short text, a Swedenborg-Emerson-Whitman connection is perceived. The question is whether this observation can be further developed. There seem to be grounds for comparison. Emory Holloway, the well-informed editor of *The Uncollected Poetry and Prose of Walt Whitman*, remarked in a note that 'There can be little doubt that Swedenborg had a strong influence on Whitman, as likewise he had on Emerson'.[6]

In the following, I will examine the trinomial Swedenborg-Emerson-Whitman connection in some detail, and especially the more direct Swedenborg-Whitman relation, to see if this can be of any importance whatsoever to the Whitman reader and to the understanding of his conception of words and objects, images and reality.

*

Both Emerson and Whitman dreamed of reproducing the expressive power of things, the omnipresent yet silent *logoi*, the poetry of nature. In their New England world a freshly built vision of Adam's primal language arose; the expressive power within things themselves and their inner essence and their meaning was reborn, revealed. It was this dream of Eden and Adamite language that Whitman framed:

> A SONG of the rolling earth, and of words according,
> Were you thinking that those were the words, those upright lines?
>   those curves, angles, dots?
> No, those are not the words, the substantial words are in the ground
>   and sea,
> They are in the air, they are in you...[7]

Whitman belonged to a generation that experienced humanity as liberated from the coils of original sin and allowed to return to the lost paradise. It now stood face to face with Nature herself, with responsibility for a world destined to elevate itself to Eden,

> To THE garden the world anew ascending.

We are 'Children of Adam'.[8] 'Here's for the plain old Adam', announced Emerson; Adam should give things their names again. Every human being is latently a new Adam. The Adamite era is here and now:

> ...in the new-born millions,
> The perfect Adam lives.[9]

When Emerson delivered his six lectures on 'The Times' at the Library Society in New York in 1842, the young editor of the New York journal *The Aurora,* Walter Whitman, was on the spot as reporter. In his lecture on 'The Poet', Emerson surprisingly stated:

> After Dante, and Shakespeare, and Milton, there came no grand poet until Swedenborg, in a corner of Europe, hitherto uncelebrated, sung the wonders of man's heart in

strange prose poems which he called Heaven and Hell, the Apocalypse Revealed, the Doctrine of Marriage, Celestial Secrets and so on, and which rivalled in depth and sublimity, and in their power to agitate this human heart—this lover of the wild and wonderful—any song of these tuneful predecessors. Slowly but surely the eye and ear of men are turning to feed on that wonderful intellect.[10]

Focusing on the symbolic, Emerson declared that 'All things are symbols. We say of man that he is grass...'. Whitman reviewed the lecture, writing, 'The lecture was one of the richest and most beautiful compositions, both for its manner and style, we have ever heard anywhere, at any time'.[11]

Whitman mentioned Swedenborg by name in two of his works—*Democratic Vistas* (1871) and *November Boughs* (1883). In *November Boughs* Swedenborg appears together with historical notables such as Frederick the Great, Junius, Voltaire, Rousseau, Linné, Herschel, and Goethe. In the prose work *Democratic Vistas* Whitman approaches the literary pertinence of the mystic. He states:

[that the]culmination and fruit of literary artistic expression, and its final fields of pleasure for the human soul, are in metaphysics, including the mysteries of the spiritual world, the soul itself, and the question of the immortal continuation of our identity. In all ages, the mind of man has brought up here—and always will...In this sublime literature the religious tone, the consciousness of mystery, the recognition of the future, of the unknown, of Deity over and under all, and of the divine purpose, are never absent, but indirectly give tone to all.

Even though these works are sometimes aesthetically defective, they are the highlights of world literature, since such 'poetry' towers up to literature's real heights and elevations like great mountains of the earth:

The altitude of literature and poetry has always been religion—and always will be. The Indian Vedas, the Nackas of Zoroaster, the Talmud of the Jews, the Old Testament, the Gospel of Christ and His disciples, Plato's works, the Koran of Mohammed, the

Edda of Snorro, and so on toward our own day, to Swedenborg, and to the invaluable contributions of Leibniz, Kant, and Hegel.[12]

There are other examples to show that America's most influential poet of the nineteenth century valued Swedenborg. Among some manuscripts at Duke University a newspaper clipping is preserved on 'The New Jerusalem' together with a page where Whitman, probably in 1857 or 1858, has taken down some of his thoughts regarding Swedenborg. It is a Swedenborg article written by Whitman. He especially observes how strangely unknown Swedenborg was in his time—neither Voltaire nor Rousseau noticed him. Whitman claims that Swedenborg's mission was one of major historical significance:

He is a precursor, in some sort of great differences between past thousands of years, and future thousands. [13]

Here we are also faced with the prophetic optimism that is the keynote of Whitman's writings, an ecstatic homage to life, man, and the times; the world will be reborn before our eyes and we will retrieve the divine nature of things—these prospects are open to all of us. Like Sampson Reed and Waldo Emerson, Whitman believed in the progress of science and society, but he thought the contemporary scientist too intellectual and devoid of the awareness of divine providence and meaning.

Enthusiastically drawn to a democratic idea of equality, founded upon metaphysics, he also defended the right of the individual against the claims and limits of the state, of customs and legislation, and became a radical defender of human rights, for instance in the Civil War era. For the same reason he also combined a trust in the common man with a belief in the existence of superhuman insight and wisdom. He exalted the Self and the I in all of us, and glorified our body and the sensual world as originally divine and inviolable. He preached freedom within the limits of natural law and wanted to guide humanity en route to a new Eden where we might revive our divine nature and recapture the language of our world. In 'Song of Myself' he hails humanity. Essentially the title, as well as the message, is identical with that of *Salut au monde!*

A Reader in Hieroglyphics

Leaves of Grass is a reading in the hieroglyphic text of nature, of which man is a part. The grass is *a uniform hieroglyphic,* a symbolic writing, which signifies an omnipresence of seething life, among all peoples, in all humans. It means: 'Sprouting alike in broad zones and narrow zones, Growing among black folks as among white, Kanuck, Tuckahoe, Congressman, Cuff'. There is a spiritual inflow into all the living, and the grass symbolises humanity, ultimately the vital force itself.[14]

Echoes may be described here of the old literary myth of the divine hieroglyphics, which dates back to Plutarch and Iamblichos and became current in Renaissance Neoplatonism and occultism; the history of hieroglyphic Bibles, storybooks, and picture puzzles; Champollion's deciphering of the Rosetta stone in the 1820s; the ancient history of allegory and analogy; but no less Emerson's well-known description of Swedenborg's conception of the world as a 'a grammar of hieroglyphs'.[15] Emerson's early usage of the word 'hieroglyph' gradually became tinged with Correspondential vision. The origin, no doubt, for this impulse came from his Swedenborgian friend Sampson Reed. Reed's interest in these matters is obvious from his contributions to the Boston journal *The New Jerusalem Magazine*, where he published a paper on Egyptian hieroglyphics in 1830. The main source of this interest was Swedenborg's attempt at an outline and system-atisation of the connections between things and words. It was published in a treatise called *Clavis hieroglyphica* (1744; posthumously published in 1784). The first American edition of that *Hieroglyphic Key* appeared in 1813 (*Halcyon Luminary*, Baltimore). Thus, the 'hieroglyphic' connection was profoundly Swedenborgian.

A similar source of major importance was the French Swedenborgian Guillaume Œgger, whose book on *The True Messiah* had left many traces in the basic outline of Emerson's philosophy in *Nature* (1836). Œgger's remarkable work *Le Vrai Messie, ou l'Ancien et le Nouveau Testaments examinés d'après les principes de la langue de la nature* (Paris, 1829), was an attempt to interpret the Holy Bible by means of the Book of Nature, translating things into thoughts and notions, and the other way round. This interplay of exegetics and ontology was derived from the old idea that The Author has written two books—the Word and the World—in corresponding hieroglyphs. Emerson read Elizabeth Palmer Peabody's manuscript translation, *The True Messiah* (published at Boston, 1842) already in 1835.[16]

According to Œgger and Swedenborg, God had endowed Adam with the faculty of reading the ideographic names of the creatures from their physical forms, so that he could recognise the significant and realise the meaning from the design. This tongue, which is the nature of things, now once again can be interpreted; Œgger presents a 'hieroglyphic key', based on Swedenborg. Œgger's list is basically a short dictionary of Correspondences, compiled from Swedenborg's exegetical and theosophical works, and the *Clavis hieroglyphica* is dimly seen in the background. He summarises and exemplifies the Doctrine of Correspondences, laying claims to its universal applicability. Thus man himself is the divine written in cipher: 'Man is the true hieroglyphic of the Divinity', infinitely detailed even in his corporeal existence, 'since his material form itself, is but the emblem of his moral being' (the entry 'God' in *Hieroglyphic Keys*). This approach to the human condition reverberates throughout Emerson's poetical universe. In the prologue to *Nature*: 'Every man's condition is a solution in hieroglyphic to those inquiries he would put'.

According to Œgger's *Hieroglyphic Keys*, or grouping of Correspondences, the two most important faculties of man are 'Goodness' and 'Knowledge' (Swedenborg's *bonum* and *scientia*); *God* is 'Love' and 'Truth'; the *Sun* in our world is 'heat' and 'light' (corresponding to the Divine Love and Wisdom of the heavens); the *Wind* announces wherever it advances 'the invisible action of a hidden God': it is 'spirit'.

This linguistic insight struck Emerson like lightning and was immediately turned into literary imagery. In the prophetic conclusion of *Nature,* the revolutionary impact of the spirit is described:

The sordor and filths of nature, the sun shall dry up, and the wind exhale.

Whitman preaches the new language, the regained Adamic perception. In 'A Song of the Rolling Earth' he writes:

I swear I begin to see little or nothing in audible words,
All merges toward the presentation of the unspoken meanings of
    the earth.

Toward him who sings the songs of the body and of the truths of
 the earth,
Toward him who makes the dictionaries of words that print cannot
 touch.

A constant theme in *Leaves of Grass* is the strange connections between the I and the World, the outward and the inward:

Locations and times—what is it in me that meets them
 All, whenever and wherever, and makes me at home?
Forms, colors, densities, odors—what is it in me
 that corresponds to them [17]

When writing 'Good-Bye My Fancy' (1891), completed on his deathbed, Whitman was many times convinced of the concurrent text: 'In every object, mountain, tree, and star —in every birth and life[...] A mystic cipher waits infolded'.

For the same reason Emerson (as did Sampson Reed) wrote: 'my garden is my dictionary', 'life is our dictionary', and in the 'Prospects' of *Nature* declare that we are all Adam's equals. That prospect was one of 'an original relation to the universe', a state of mind when the different planes of reality and our awareness once again coincide and everything suddenly becomes 'transparent', reveals its inner nature, its truth. The Concord philosophy rings out as hymn and formula in the poem 'Correspondences', written by Christopher Pearse Cranch (1813-1892) for Emerson's and Margaret Fuller's *The Dial* at the outset of the 1840s:

Lost to man was the key of those sacred hieroglyphics,—
 Stolen away by sin,—till with Jesus restored.
Now with infinite pains we here and there spell out a letter;
 Now and then will the sense feebly shine through the dark.
When we perceive the light which breaks through the visible symbol,
 What exultation is ours! we the discovery have made!

Yet is the meaning the same as when Adam lived sinless in Eden

Only long-hidden it slept and now again is restored.[18]

The key opens the door of meaning by way of symbolic signs or signatures: the thing, the image. Therefore 'indirection' is a keyword in both Whitman and Emerson. The grammar of the universe is searched for.

*

Emerson wrote a powerful and well-informed essay on Swedenborg, the scientist and the 'mystic,' two epithets which for Emerson always were prestige words. That colourful piece from the second half of the 1840s shows the remarkable intensity of both his fascination and his reaction. Its critical points were but sharpened by the fact that it was rumoured that Mr and Mrs Emerson, and she especially, were Swedenborgians.[19] Opposition is the token of impact, the idiom of the dialogue. Swedenborg made profound impressions which could not be swept away. Nor did he leave Whitman unaffected or unconcerned. In the preceding remarks I have also tried to show that Whitman, at least for some time, took an interest in Swedenborg, and that there are several—if only ambiguous—affinities between his views and Swedenborg's ideas.

Here it can be added that Dr Richard Maurice Bucke, in his analytical biography on his friend Walt Whitman (a book which Whitman partly wrote himself), adduced a document which is of some relevance to us, a private testimony. In a memorandum written for the biography, Helen E Price, who made Whitman's acquaintance in 1856, told that Whitman frequently met with one of her neighbours. That 'Mr A' (John Arnold), was 'a man of wide knowledge and the most analytical mind of anyone I ever knew. He was a Swedenborgian'. Whitman and Arnold often had long discussions and conversations. Helen Price remembered Whitman as an *exalté*. According to her, his distinctive feature was his profound spirituality: 'his *religious sentiment* [...] pervades and dominates his life'.[20]

Partly inspired by Arnold too, Whitman seems to have attended New Church meetings and studied Swedenborg's life and writings.[21] This way we may understand the earlier mentioned article and manuscript fragment on Swedenborg, where the seer is regarded as a kind of spiritual pioneer or regenerator—which appears to be a sketch for an essay

Whitman wrote for the Brooklyn *Daily Times* in 1858.[22] In that comprehensive article, entitled 'Who was Swedenborg?', Whitman claimed that Swedenborg, among whose followers 'are some of the leading minds of our nation', will probably 'make the deepest and broadest mark upon the religions of future ages here, of any man that ever walked the earth'.[23]

From these pieces of writing, and from the extensive conversations with Horace Traubel during the many years of failing health in Camden, where he spent his last nineteen years, it is clear that Whitman time and again through the decades pondered upon the strange phenomenon Emanuel Swedenborg, including also the Swedish mystic's strange illumination and divine initiation — a historic event that, according to Whitman, marked the emergence of the individual consciousness in modern religious thought. Whitman observed the 'somewhat comical', 'most unromantic and vulgar' commencement of Swedenborg's very rare 'ineffable privilege': Swedenborg first came into rapport with the Lord and the spiritual world by eating a dinner at an inn in London.[24]

This certainly struck the positive and sensual Whitman's fancy. Even more than his master Emerson, he always tried to envisage the divine or transcendent qualities and meanings of the commonplace and the low. Whitman, who also paid attention to Swedenborg's perception of the Correspondences between religious ecstasy and erotic desire, observed, 'I find Swedenborg confirmed in all my experience. It is a peculiar discovery'.[25]

*

But there is still another observation to be added here. If Whitman drew from Swedenborgian teachings such as the Doctrine of Influx and the Doctrine of Correspondences, as Emerson did, it is possible that Swedenborgian hermeneutics in some instances can be applied to his own wordings.[26] In that case the comprehensive English dictionaries of Correspondences compiled from Swedenborg's writings by James Hindmarsh (1794) and by George Nicholson (1800) may assist us.[27] The latter work was circulated in New England in a revised edition published in Boston in 1841: *A Dictionary of Correspondences, Representatives, and Significatives, derived from the Word of the Lord.*[28] There we encounter the paradigm which is basic to all of Swedenborg's writings, according to which 'heat' is love, 'light' is truth and wisdom, 'darkness' is falsity, 'ascendancy' is an advancement towards the celestial, 'fire' is egotist love and infernal lusts; 'serpents' are sensual things, 'birds' are wandering thoughts and associations, and 'beasts' signify different affections; 'clouds' signify obscurities of the mind, whereas 'flowers' have good connotations and 'grass' signifies 'what is alive in man', which is the spiritual life force; 'leaves' are 'truths', the 'Sun' corresponds to celestial love, and 'winds' are spirits and influxes.

Then compare Emerson's use of linguistic examples and his manner of building his arguments upon such illustrations, for instance in *Nature* and in his lectures on Natural History. Emerson early used the Doctrine of Correspondences for his metaphors, and this usage abounds in many of his works, sometimes with salient similarities to the imagery and reasoning of Swedenborg's most well-known work: *A Treatise Concerning Heaven and its Wonders, and also Concerning Hell*. A copy of the 1823 London edition with Emerson's annotations is still to be seen in his extant library. Striking resemblances emerge between Emerson's and Swedenborg's philosophy of language, and in Emerson's usage.

In *Nature* (1836), Emerson enumerates a number of the aforementioned Correspond-ences in the chapter called 'Language', which illustrates the Swedenborgian paradigm of reading material and spiritual meaning at the same time.

This comparison becomes still more exciting, however, if we use this key to the enigmatic, never fully explained title of *Leaves of Grass*. If we substitute 'truths' for *Leaves,* and 'what is alive in man' for *Grass*, we then get the title:

Truths of What is Alive in Man.

Such is indeed the theme and the subject of Whitman's epoch-making book; it is that of which the Singer sings his praise.

*

Those who were the first to praise Whitman, had also read Swedenborg or New Church literature with delight. Documentary evidence shows that Whitman had done so too. As in Emerson, this reading added something to the tone and meaning of figurative language and to the conception of the real in Whitman's singular poetic diction.

NOTES

[1] Harold Bloom, *The Western Canon*, (New York, Riverhead Books, 1995), 247.

[2] *ibid*, 249, 254, 256 f., 259, 261, 264.

[3] Bloom, *Whitman* (New York, Macmillan, 1938).

[4] See especially Henry Seidel Canby, *Walt Whitman*, (Boston, 1943), 120f, and Roger Asselineau's well-informed discussion of the background of the first (1855) edition: *The Evolution of Walt Whitman*, (Cambr. Mass., 1960). Suzanne Poirier perceived the echoes of Emerson and Transcendentalism in Whitman's symbolism: ' "A Song of the Rolling Earth" as Transcendental and Poetic Theory', *Walt Whitman Review*, Vol. 22 (June, 1976), 67-74. As pointed out by Ralph Rusk, the printing of Emerson's letter, with its public use by Whitman, 'was perhaps an event of greater importance in the history of American literature than the printing of any other letter has ever been', *The Letters of Ralph Waldo Emerson*, 1939, Vol. IV, 520. Emerson's letter to Whitman was written on July 21, 1855.

[5] See Roger Asselineau, *The Evolution of Walt Whitman*, (Cambr., Mass.: Harvard University Press, 1960), I, 75.

[6] Emory Holloway, (ed.) *The Uncollected Poetry and Prose of Walt Whitman,* (Garden City, New York, 1921 and London: Heineman, 1922), II, 16n.

[7] The introductory strophe of 'A Song of the Rolling Earth' (1856), printed in the edition of *Leaves of Grass* in which he praised and cited Emerson. *The Complete Poetry and Prose of Walt Whitman as Prepared by Him for the Deathbed Edition*, with an introduction by Malcolm Cowley, (NY 1948), Vol. I, 216.

[8] 'To the Garden of the World' (1860), first section of 'Children of Adam' in *Leaves of Grass (The Complete Poetry and Prose)* I, 114.

[9] *The Complete Works of Ralph Waldo Emerson*, (Centenary Edition, Boston and New York, 1903-1904), Vol. I, 76, Vol. IX, 283 ('Promise'), Vol. X, 137; Joel Porte, ed., *Emerson in his Journals* (1982), 99, and chapter 'Reorientation 1833-34'; R W B Lewis, *The American Adam: Innocence, Tragedy, and Tradition in the Nineteenth Century* (1955), prologue and ch. I:2, 'The New Adam: Holmes and Whitman'. For another perspective on the creative mission in the New World's pristine outlying land: Henry Nash Smith, *Virgin Land* (1970), ch. 'Walt Whitman and Manifest Destiny'. On the first and last Adam—the physical preceding the spiritual—I Cor. 15:45.

[10] *The Early Lectures of Ralph Waldo Emerson*, III, 352, 361: The Times Series 'The Poet'.

[11] Gay Wilson Allen, *Waldo Emerson*, (New York: Penguin Books, 1982), 400f.; Joseph Jay Rubin & Charles H Brown, (eds.), *Walt Whitman of the New York Aurora, Editor at Twenty-two: A Collection of Recently Discovered Writings*, (Pennsylvania State College: Bald Eagle Press, 1950), 105. The full text of the lecture Whitman reported: *The Early Lectures of Ralph Waldo Emerson*, III, 347-365. Some passages from that lecture on 'The Poet' Emerson later

used in the essays 'The Poet', 'Eloquence', and 'Poetry and Imagination'.

[12] Walt Whitman, *The Complete Poetry and Prose*, II, 470 resp. 263. Textual note: the spelling is that of the Editio Princeps and most later editions. Read 'Naçkas,' 'Snorre,' 'Leibniz'.

[13] Manuscript 35, #25; see *The Collected Writings of Walt Whitman. Notebooks and unpublished Prose Manuscripts,* ed. E F Grier, (New York, 1984), Vol. VI, 2034-2035. The clipping identified by Stovall (*The Foreground*, 156, n. 17) as No. 278 in Bucke's *Notes and Fragments*.

[14] Whitman, *Collected Writings*, VII:34—cf. John T Irwin, *American Hieroglyphics. The Symbol of the Egyptian Hieroglyphics in the American Renaissance,* (Baltimore & London, 1980), 19f.

[15] John T Irwin, *American Hieroglyphics,* 30 ff.; E Iversen, *The myth of Egypt and its hieroglyphs in European tradition*,(Copenhagen, 1961); W A Clouston, *Hieroglyphic Bibles: Their Origin and History,* (Glasgow, 1894); Sampson Reed, 'Egyptian Hieroglyphics', *New Jerusalem Magazine* Vol. IV (1830-31), Oct., 69. That the world to Swedenborg appeared as only 'a grammar of hieroglyphs' Emerson stated in *Representative Men* in 1850, i.e., five years before *Leaves of Grass* (*The Complete Works of Ralph Waldo Emerson,* IV, 142).

[16] The excerpts are to be found in his Journal B, 1835, i.e., the year before his first book was published: *The Journals and Miscellaneous Notebooks of Ralph Waldo Emerson,* (Cambr., Mass, 1960-1982), Vol. V, 65-69. On Abbé Œgger, see: Karl-Erik Sjödén, *Swedenborg en France*, Stockholm 1985. On the Middle Age and Renaissance ideas behind this kind of hermeneutics: Michel Foucault, *The Order of Things: An Archaeology of the Human Sciences.* The 'World Of Man' series, Ed. R D Laing, (New York, 1973), 25ff. & passim.

[17] This theme is discussed in Christoffer Collins, *The Uses of Observation*, (The Hague and Paris, 1971), chap. IV.

[18] Perry Miller, ed., *The Transcendentalists*, 1979 (1950): 388; see also 'Correspondence' in the useful index.

[19] Ralph L Rusk, *The Life of Ralph Waldo Emerson*, (New York, 1949), 215, 220, 363: Lidian Emerson (Lydia Jackson) in fact once (during the lecture tour in England in the late 1840's) introduced herself as a Christian and Swedenborgian.

[20] Richard Maurice Bucke, *Walt Whitman*, (New York and London, 1970 (1883)), 26-32. The part Whitman played in the production of the book is shown by Quentin Anderson/Stephen Railton, *Walt Whitman's Autograph Revision of the Analysis of Leaves of Grass (For Dr R M Bucke's Walt Whitman),* (New York, 1974). Whitman's 'indirection': 21, 76 (a characteristic term culled from Emerson: 'all goes by indirection', *The Complete Works of Ralph Waldo Emerson,* VII,81). Whitman's spirituality and his religiosity are obvious, even though (or still more, 'since') he considered historical churches and creeds obstacles to the divine, as did Emerson. See Whitman's sketches for a series of lectures on religion: *Walt Whitman's Workshop: A Collection of Unpublished Manuscripts*, edited with an introduction and notes by Clifton Joseph Furness, (New York, 1964), 39-53, 218-221. Paul Zweig's *Walt Whitman: The Making*

of the Poet (1984) encounters the religious dimension, and even more so does David Kuebrich in *Minor Prophecy: Walt Whitman's New American Religion* (1989). Kuebrich reminds us that Whitman in his time was esteemed as a religious seer as much as a poet, and views him as a prophet.

[21] See Justin Kaplan's very informative biography *Walt Whitman: A Life,* (New York, 1980), 231f.

[22] *Daily Times,* June 15, 1858. Emory Holloway, ed., *The Uncollected Poetry and Prose of Walt Whitman*, (Garden City, New York, 1921), Vol. II, 16-18. Justin Kaplan, *op. cit.*, 192 f. Similarities between Whitman and Swedenborg were pointed out by Frederik Schyberg, *Walt Whitman*, (Copenhagen, 1933), 12, 72, 88, 278 f.

[23] Holloway (1921) II.

[24] Kaplan (1980), 192; 'Who was Swedenborg?' Holloway (1921), 16. Whitman's account of Swedenborg's initial vision, in the *Daily Times* article of 1858, shows that he was familiar with the historical version taken down in the bank executive Carl Robsahm's memoirs (1782). Swedenborg never told the whole story of the occurrences in London in 1745 except verbally to his friend Robsahm. Robsahm's anecdotes were introduced in the USA by a fellow student of Emerson at Harvard, Nathaniel Hobart, in his documentary *Life of Emanuel Swedenborg*, published at Boston in 1831. Robsahm's account was published *in extenso* in the enlarged edition of Hobart's book issued in 1845, and in the edition printed and distributed in New York in 1850. Hobart's *Life* was the most important Swedenborg biography to Emerson when he wrote his influential lecture and essay 'Swedenborg; or, the Mystic' (written and revised 1845-1849 and published in *Representative Men*, 1850). I have discussed the pertinence of Robsahm and Hobart to the reception of Swedenborg in the preface to my annotated critical edition of Robsahm's memoirs: Carl Robsahm, *Anteckningar om Swedenborg*, (Stockholm 1989). The internal evidence here shown indicates that Whitman was familiar with Hobart's documentary *Life of Swedenborg*; at least Hobart was evidently the source—directly or indirectly—of Whitman's account.

[25] Horace Traubel, *With Walt Whitman in Camden*. (Vol. V.) April 8 - September 14, 1889, ed. (Gertrude Traubel, Carbondale, Illinois, 1964), 376.

[26] Both Emerson and Whitman frequently seem to cite the teachings on spiritual influx, but their understanding of such 'inflow' is rather vague and can be derived from various sources. Swedenborg's seminal 'Doctrine of influx' was first introduced on the American scene by the publication of 'A Treatise on the Nature of Influx', a translation of *De Commercio Animæ et Corporis,* published in the *Halcyon Luminary*, Vol. II, (Baltimore, New York, 1813).

[27] Both dictionaries are based upon Gabriel Beyer's gigantic pioneer work *Index Initialis in Opera Swedenborgii theologica,* (Amsterdam, 1779). Compare also William L Worcester, *The Language of Parable: A Key to the Bible,* (New York, 1984 (1892)), and Alice Spiers Sechrist, *A Dictionary of Bible Imagery: A Guide for Bible Readers*, (New York, 1981 (1973)).

[28] A second edition was published in 1847, the fourth edition in 1863, the 9th ed. in 1887... Reprinted in a new edition (the fourteenth) by the Swedenborg Foundation, (New York, 1988).

Subjectivity and Truth: Strindberg and Swedenborg[1]

Lars Bergquist

'S implicity would seem to be less perfect than complexity, but simplicity, from which complexity derived, is more perfect'.

This quotation is from Emanuel Swedenborg's *Divine Providence*[2] and serves as a motto in August Strindberg's book *Religiös Renässans, eller Religion mot Teologi* [*Religious Renaissance*],[3] a collection of essays published in 1910, two years before the author's death.

The idea that simplicity possesses greater perfection than complexity may be seen to epitomize both Swedenborg and Strindberg's scientific and religious search: *Solve et coagula!*—that is, break up that which is complex, and make coherent that which is fragmentary! This can be seen in the attempt to derive pure gold in the alchemists' chemical marriage, as well as the simple truth of the obedient correspondence of form whose content derives from the union between spirit and matter. Applied to the Christian conceptual world, this idea implied a repudiation of all formalized orthodoxy and the promotion of the primacy of spirit over theology.

Strindberg was brought up in a Lutheran Christian home, and received a sound knowledge of the Bible and Lutheran dogma from his parents and the religious instruction of his schooling. As a young man he was religiously committed and, with episcopal permission, preached on several occasions in provincial churches. The title of his autobiography, *Tjänstekvinnans son* [*The Son of a Servant*],[4] indicates his intimate knowledge of the biblical world. He sees himself as Ishmael—Abraham's son by the servant Hagar—born of the father of the faith but nevertheless outside the Holy Covenant.

On approaching the age of fifty this religious commitment began to intensify, eventually forming a screen upon which he superimposed the major part of his work. The 'Inferno crisis' of 1894 to 1896 was a turning-point. Strindberg embarked on a Swedenborgian path which he was to follow, more or less faithfully, during his last fifteen years. The crisis marked the departure into a radical regeneration of his writing and, according to Gunnar Brandell, a well-known Swedish literary historian, the 'most significant innovation in our literature'. Personal and moral issues came increasingly to the forefront with a constant need for soul-searching and the subsequent insight into his own moral frailty. At the same time, his dramatic art assumed a lyrical note, partly due to his new vitalistic and symbolistic outlook. He wanted to regard heaven and earth, and even life and death, as a single whole in which everything, when studied more closely, disintegrated into seperate entities which reflected and elucidated each other. Reality and dream were mingled in a view of the world as being the mysterious work of art of an invisible master.

Monism, vitalism, symbolism and losing oneself in 'the sea of the world of visions' were characteristic of the age. Strindberg had, of course, noted the swing of the pendulum away from the naturalism of the 1880s. As well as the 'spirit of the age', there was his own personal crisis of over-exertion, despair and pangs of conscience over two failed marriages and children made fatherless by their respective break-ups. Bad finances and the feeling that his creative power was on the ebb were also part of the picture. This crisis, coupled with the influence of new intellectual currents, paved the way for his final creative period incorporating two interconnected and central areas: alchemy and his interest in Emanuel Swedenborg.

Alchemy is based on a comprehensive view of combining the spiritual and the material which is linked to the Aristotelian idea that everything can be reduced to a single substance, a basic *essentia* with varying attributes. In this view the universe is animated and is always developing towards greater perfection. In the same way that the evil man can be reformed, so lead can be induced to set aside its heavy character and be turned into gold. In a neo-Platonic spirit, such a transformation was thought to be facilitated by the fact that all 'living' things—even metals and minerals—long for refinement and sigh like the animals in Paul's *Epistles* (Romans 8: 18-25), i.e. that which was once united strives for a new union in a 'chemical marriage': matter is human, it has a memory and therefore a psychology.

Strindberg described his alchemical experiments in *Inferno*[5] and numerous journal articles. The classical idea of the temporary nature and changeability of matter fascinated him for two reasons: in the first instance because, at least at times, he thought he could make a new career as a scientist—he was not entangled in the atomistic and mechanistic approach to science of the period, and had an unbiased eye. In the second instance, he recognised its great poetic qualities which would have appealed to his sensibilities as a writer. There was perhaps an opportunity here to prove that all variety comes under a single principle, that the universe is animated and that man's creative possibilities are unlimited.

During 1895 to 1896, in his hotel rooms in Paris, he tried to bring about the metal-lurgical transmutation attempted in vain for centuries, first according to the main lines of the old formulas, then by speculating on the numerical ratios between the elements. He published papers and theses on the subject but eventually gave up: eczema on his hands, lack of recognition and bad business may be put forward as tangible external reasons. Presumably his experiments had already provided him with important impulses which, together with other areas of study, were much later to give his writing a special and distinctive tension. Just as separated chemical substances once united longed for reunion, so he came to see the whole of life as chaos, founded on a mysterious longing for order. Human problems, the mysteries of existence, were placed in a force field, the appearance of which changed with the perspective of the observer.

His scientific Romanticism was transformed into occultism and mysticism during the 'Inferno crisis' mainly as a result of his study of Emanuel Swedenborg, the grand master of modern European symbolism. Swedenborg conceived of man as a constantly creative being, whose ideas and outlook were dependent on the state of the ego. The symbolists considered landscape to be a state of mind. But landscape was not enough for Swedenborg.

Everything—Christian faith or lack of faith, the texts of books, the appearance of people, life on earth in its entirety—acquired meaning and form according to our inner mental state at the moment of observation. He extrapolated this relation into eternity: in his eyes heaven and hell were never consequences but different states of mind (*status animae*). Our predominant love in this life—our main state during our decades on earth—determines our place in the next life: in other words, it is our love that determines whether we end up in the subjective states of mind called heaven or hell. Sin is its own punishment, writes Strindberg in his *There are Crimes and Crimes* [6] re-stating one of Swedenborg's fundamental ideas. Similarly, joy and peace are inherent in good and especially in the good deed. We choose our roles ourselves, now and for eternity.

Strindberg's entire literary production from the 'Inferno crisis' to his death in 1912 is marked by his study of Swedenborg. He had, as mentioned, received an old-fashioned Christian upbringing, and had been taught to think in Christian categories such as: sin/ grace; guilt/forgiveness; suffering/perfection; rejection/love. Having already been influenced by the theosophy and occultism of the late nineteenth century, the study of his mystical fellow-countryman consolidated and enriched his view of our existence as a mysterious palimpsest, in which layer upon layer of obscure, fragmentary texts intimated hidden connections in an animated world.

Presumably it was the literary qualities and possibilities in Swedenborg's works which first caught his attention. A monistic, comprehensive view, and the conviction that the spirit and the body are one, had been self-evident to Strindberg during his alchemical period. The inorganic was in actual fact organic: the ice-ferns on the window-panes caused by cold and vapour formed themselves into the counterparts of the living plants. Now, thanks to his study of Swedenborg, the idea was elevated to a higher plane. Life on earth is a battlefield, not only for mortals of flesh and blood, but also for the spirits of the dead—the spirits which have been transformed into states of mind after death. There are no distances between similar states in the spiritual world, and no time. Inspired by Swedenborg, Strindberg lets the oscillations of his dramatic characters between good and evil, truth and falsehood, be strengthened by demons, 'powers', and 'corrective spirits'. He had personal experiences of both bad and good spirits. The demons visit him with the aim of purging him. He is already being punished in life on earth. But there are also guardian angels—Providence intervenes with constantly active, invisible hands.

In *A Dream Play*[7] we encounter the idea—which is typical of Swedenborg and all mystics—of the dream, vision and intuition as an inspired source of knowledge of a different nature from that of discursive analysis. The whole play is in the form of a dream about a dream; in which one of the key images is the castle in the writer's dream, a castle which grows like a flower. The plant does not like the earthly dirt, but must reach up into the light to bloom; and the same applies to the poet's edifice. Swedenborg's conception of man's calling to light and clarity in a devotion to God, in which egoism is overcome, occurs throughout the drama. But here, as in *To Damascus*,[8] Strindberg adopts his own attitudes towards justice. His characters mirror his own protest: there is perhaps a 'duty to seek freedom in the light', he writes, but submission is impossible for one unjustly punished, wronged by life. Swedenborg had surrendered to the divine during the *Journal of Dreams*[9] crisis. For Strindberg and his characters such a compromise or surrender is impossible. 'We are unjustly punished!'—the idea appears as a refrain in the chorus of the earthly captives. Jacob's wrestling and Titan's struggle symbolize his attitude throughout his final years.

But justification in the face of an unjust fate must, of course, be coupled with remorse for the wrongs one has committed and the continuous task of improving the self. His study of Swedenborg gave Strindberg a key concept, which first appears during the 'Inferno' period and is then found in both his drama and prose until his death. This is Swedenborg's *vastatio* or devastation: a sort of purgatory. Even the man who has lived honourably must, it says in Swedenborg's *Arcana Caelestia*,[10] be freed from evils and deceits before going to heaven. This purge or 'dispersion' may be short or it may be long and it takes various shapes, from torments or agony to mild reformations. Strindberg himself quoted from §1108 of *Arcana Caelestia*:

Some are kept in a condition halfway between being awake and being asleep, and think very little. By turns so to speak they wake up and remember what they have thought and done during their lifetime, only to slip back again into the halfway condition between being awake and being asleep. In this way they were vastated.

Penance, remorse, and pangs of conscience were Strindberg's main themes, coupled with the painful reflection that guilt already takes the form of devastation in life on earth. This 'review of life' usually occurs somewhere between the age of 40 and 50, 'a summing-up at the solstice', as it is referred to in *A Blue Book*;[11]

> Everything past is beginning to be added up, and the debit side shows a terrifying figure. Scenes from one's former life unroll as in a panorama, are placed in a new light... everything down to the last detail is brought to light.

The Swedenborgian idea of dreams and intuition as a source of knowledge often appears in Strindberg's texts after the crisis. In an Introductory Note in *A Dream Play*, he writes about dreams as being at once incoherent and logical:

> The characters split, double, multiply, evaporate, condense, disperse, assemble. But one consciousness rules over them all, that of the dreamer; for him there are no secrets, no illogicalities, no scruples, no laws. He neither acquits nor condemns, but merely relates...

Dream is a tormentor, often painful, he writes: awakening can be a relief. But even waking life is full of torments, dreamlike and inexplicable. Perhaps death is the only release, an awakening to a longed-for clarity of vision.

Strindberg came to see life as an imperfect reflection of a higher existence. In this higher existence there might be found an explanation for everything, but here on earth the reflection is mysterious and incoherent. Here he is in agreement with Swedenborg, his 'teacher and guide' and the analogical and anagogical 'thinking in symbols' which Swedenborg had in common with Augustine and Dante. But, as I have already mentioned, Strindberg's constant protests and revolts make him unable to attain Swedenborg's calm and reassuring trust. Moments of literary inspiration seem to be the exception: he speaks of 'the surging joy of conception' but as soon as he commits it to paper it becomes something else——'to write is to diminish!'. As such he is crushed by a constant gnashing of teeth: 'But it is this very act of not being crushed which is culture, philosophy, music', wrote Vilhelm Ekelund, the Swedish moralist, apropos Strindberg. 'The Nordic people never see anything but the unphilosophical'. A calm, settled and serene attitude to life was not granted to Strindberg until the final stage of his life.

The Swedenborgian doctrine of states, in which time and space are abolished and the distances between individuals with kindred states of mind are removed, is constant in *A Dream Play*. Strindberg allows the scenes to merge into one another as the ideas roam, and the characters gather in groups somewhat like the spirits in Swedenborg's heaven and hell. Everyone sees what he wants to see, the rooms take their colour and character from the inhabitant's thoughts and mood. 'You believe only evil and therefore receive only evil', says the Beggar to the Stranger in *To Damascus*. This is Swedenborg's doctrine to the letter. Streets, houses, squares and parks in the heavens, which Swedenborg visits as an explorer, serve as functions of the thoughts and dispositions of the good spirits——of the angels. The same was true of the stench and the torture-instruments of hell. The wealthy men of pleasure are already on earth, now, in their self-chosen asylum, writes Strindberg in *A Dream Play*. 'Look at him!', says the Quarantine Master at Skamsund and points to a gentleman on a mechanical exercise apparatus: 'That fellow is lying on the guillotine. He's drunk so much Hennessey brandy that they had to run his spine through the mangle'.

The right disposition of will and love, in turn, conditions our outlook by enabling us to see the correspondences pervading the world. Everything here on earth is a reflection of something higher, wrote Swedenborg, and in book after book he described how words and objects made hieroglyphic references to things beyond and above themselves. Life on earth in all its manifestations, or *figurae*, consists of incomplete, fragmentary images of a higher, spiritual reality. This also applies to the fates individual people make for themselves, and to a very high degree to a large part of the biblical texts. Strindberg studied eagerly, but seems mainly to have used the Doctrine of Correspondences as a justification for his view of the animated and mysteriously connected nature of existence. But he prefers to keep to 'horizontal' Correspondences, and refrains on the whole from the vertical aspect. From *Inferno* onwards his life and works are full of such 'horizontal' observations, which he interprets as signs from above. A walnut kernel becomes the hands of a child clasped in prayer: a symbol of his neglect of his own children. Flower-heads become human faces——threatening, warning or encouraging. '*Numen Adest*', God is here, wrote Carl Linnaeus on the wall of his house, at Hammarby near Uppsala. Strindberg shared that opinion, but did not equal Swedenborg's systemisation as far as the forms of existence were concerned.

The Blue Books were begun in 1906, and the last volume was published after his death in 1912. The writer himself saw them as his 'life's synthesis', and were therefore dedicated to Emanuel Swedenborg, 'my teacher and guide'. The books describe, in short passages, Strindberg's views on the absolute subjectivity of human knowledge, and what he considers to be the *tabula rasa* of the science of that time. We thus see what we want to see, in the spirit of Swedenborg. What is more, we see what we *can* see, by means of organs which themselves shape our vision. Bees build their honeycombs because their facetted eyes see everything as cellular structures. Man thinks the moon is round, because his eyes are round; '...my sight weakened by eyes, my hearing muffled by ears, and my thought, my light, airy thought, prisoner in the fat windings of a brain', complains Indra's daughter and God's representative in *A Dream Play*. The world is a mystery, the secret of which can only be divined by the dreamer and the writer.

'I'm pasting, I'm pasting', cries the maid Kristin in *A Dream Play*. She is pasting over the joints of the inner windows and cutting off the characters from the sky and fresh air. 'I'm suffocating', says Indra's Daughter, who is married to a lawyer disfigured by all the evil which has poured out of his clients. The panting breaths behind the sealed inner windows are perhaps an image of the Strindbergian paradox, more full of tension and contradictions than Swedenborg's gentle and exact preaching on the levels, schools and states of animated life. Swedenborg, Strindberg and the whole symbolistic school considered subjectivity to be the truth. And perhaps they are right. At any rate, surely it is only in subjectivity that we come closer to what we are accustomed to call the truth.

NOTES

[1] This paper was first given as a talk at University College London, 1994.

[2] E Swedenborg, *Divine Providence,* current English edition: Trans. W C Dick. (The Swedenborg Society, 1949). This quotation is most likely a paraphrase of §6.1. Translation by Lars Bergquist

[3] A Strindberg, *Religious Renaissance* (*Religiös Renässans, eller Religion mot Teologi*), 1910. A collection of essays. There is no current English translation.

[4] Strindberg, *The Son of a Servant* (*Tjänstekvinnans son*), 1886. Current English edition: *The Son of a Servant, the Story of the Evolution of a Human Being, 1849-67,* trans. Evert Sprinchorn, (London: Cape, 1967).

[5] Strindberg, *Inferno* (*Inferno*). 1897. Current English edition: *Inferno/From an Occult Diary,* ed. Torsten Eklund, trans. Mary Sandbach, (Penguin Classics, October 2001).

[6] Strindberg, *There are Crimes and Crimes* (*Brott och Brott*), 1900. Current English edition: *Eight Best Plays of August Strindberg,* trans. Edwin Björkman and N Erichsen, (Duckworth, 1979).

[7] Strindberg, *A Dream Play* (*Ett Drömspell*), 1907. Current English edition: *Miss Julie and Other Plays*, trans. Michael Robinson, (Oxford University Press, 1998).

[8] Strindberg, *To Damascus* (*'Till Damaskus*). In three parts written between 1898-1904. Current English edition including all three parts: *Plays of Confession and Therapy*, trans. Walter Johnson, (University of Washington Press, 1979). Part One is available in *Plays: Three*, trans. Michael Meyer, (Methuen Drama, 1991).

[9] Swedenborg, *Journal of Dreams*. Most recent English edition: *Swedenborg's Dream Diary,* trans. Anders Hallengren with commentary by Lars Bergquist, (The Swedenborg Foundation, 2001).

[10] Swedenborg, *Arcana Caelestia*. First published in Latin between 1749-1756. Current Engish edition: *Arcana Caelestia*, trans. John Elliott, (The Swedenborg Society, 1983-1999).

[11] Strindberg, *A Blue Book* (*En Blå Bok*). *The Blue Books* were written between 1906 and the author's death in 1912. There is no current English translation.

Swedenborg and Borges: from the Mystic of the North to the Mystic *in puribus*

Emilio R Báez-Rivera

etween 10.30 in the evening until just before midnight of Monday 23rd of November 1654, Blaise Pascal (1623-1662) is overwhelmed by a vision of God in the totality of his scientific and philosophic spirit. Using a timeless metaphor he described it as a supernatural fire. On a parchment—whose language is torn asunder at the moment it tries to describe the identity of the divine presence—the word 'FEU' (FIRE), emphasised with capitalised graphemes, occupies an exclusive, privileged space within the script. It is a sketch of eternity that this celebrated scholar of emptiness and 'probabilities' essayed in a fascinating *Memorial* carefully folded and hidden in the hem of his waistcoat,[1] with the possible intention of cultivating such an unmerited gift in the secret chamber of his being. This sort of solipsism present in Pascal's tendency to silence was shared by Emanuel Swedenborg (1688-1772) and Jorge Luis Borges (1899-1986) with the reservation that Borges, as a writer of literature, made ready his intimate mystical experiences for publication.

Approximately a century after the *Memorial* of Pascal, Swedenborg, in an impeccable Swedish—although all his published works were written in Latin—wrote a travel diary published posthumously into English as *The Dream Diary* or *The Journal of Dreams*.

Here he records a series of dreams—dated 1743 and 1744—that are, without doubt, some of the most striking experiences of all his writings. Within these experiences are found the private codes of his mystical language as well as his vision/mission in the world. Even the language selected to recount these anecdotes and revelations is not arbitrary: he deliberately chooses his mother tongue to reflect on this profound and personal inner silence.[2]

It is not accidental—from a different perspective—that Borges includes the story of his first mystical experience[3] in a modest note entitled *Feeling in Death* (1928)[4] that also features in his essay *A New Refutation of Time*. In effect, this experience touched him enough for it to be republished over a period of eight years in three separate books: *The Idioms of the Argentineans* (1928); *The History of Eternity* (1936); and *Other Inquisitions* (1952). During this time he altered nothing. According to Juan Arana this confirms the view that 'we are not in front of just another experiment but an event offering a definite crystallisation of the spirit of the author'.[5] And, if this were not enough, a second mystical experience surprised him on the bridge of Avenida Constitución, above the train station in Buenos Aires, and immortalised in his enigmatic poem 'Mateo XXV, 30' (1953)[6] first published almost a decade later in his book *The Other, the Same* (1962). Utterly convinced of the mystical nature of these experiences, Borges superficially recounted them at Indiana University to Willis Barnstone in 1982,[7] at the University of Chicago to Luce López-Baralt of the same year[8] and at the Dickinson College (Carlyle, Pennsylvania) in 1983. Meanwhile, he confided in Maria Kodama the firm resolution of entering a Zen monastery in Japan for a year under the guidance of a friend who was a Buddhist monk, in order to comprehend his ecstatic experiences.[9] Unfortunately, Borges' death dashed this project. His writings have survived, nevertheless, and here tribute is paid to the Mystic of the North as one of the primary influences of Christian mysticism present in all his work.

It is possible, therefore, that Borges' admiration for Swedenborg exceeds the straight-forward allusions (both implicit and explicit) in his creative texts, as well as the deference he expresses in the 'various anthologies and written prologues to translations of Swedenborg into Spanish'.[10] They are united through the mystical experience. Let us therefore look for the presence of Swedenborg in the work of Borges beyond the simple or nominal reference.

A quick glance, in fact, will confirm the varied ways in which this presence can be found in the essays and poems. To begin with, Swedenborg appears as a voice of authority in relation to the 'illegitimate' mysticism of Pascal. For instance, in his essay 'Pascal' in *Other Inquisitions* (1952), Borges writes:

> He [Pascal] is not a mystic. He belongs to those Christians, denounced by Swedenborg, who suppose that heaven is an award and hell is a punishment: and who, through their melancholy meditations, are closed to the discourse of angels.[11]

Likewise, in the second footnote to this text, he states that 'for Swedenborg as for Böhme [...] heaven and hell are states that man looks for in freedom: they are neither a penal system nor a pious establishment'. Borges' interest in Swedenborg is further confirmed in his laudatory sonnet 'Emanuel Swedenborg' in *The Other, The Same* (1964):

> Taller than the others, this man
> Walked among them, at a distance,
> Now and then calling the angels
> By their secret names. He would see
> That which earthly eyes do not see:
> The fierce geometry, the crystal
> Labyrinth of God and the sordid
> Milling of infernal delights.
> He knew that Glory and Hell too
> Are in your soul, with all their myths;
> He knew, like the Greek, that the days
> Of time are Eternity's mirrors.
> In dry Latin he went on listing
> The unconditional Last Things.[12]

And he also features in a couple of lines of 'Otro poema de los dones' ['Another poem of gifts'] in the same book:

> Thanks I want to give to the divine
> Labyrinth of effects and causes
>
> . . .
>
> by Swedenborg,
> who used to talk with angels in the streets of London...[13]

Finally, Borges returns to the topic of Emanuel Swedenborg in the third of five lectures delivered at the University of Belgrano. Here he speaks openly about the fascinating personality of his preferred mystic, knowing he was sharing many concrete things with his spiritual ideology. From here, in turn, it is possible to trace a dialogue of the more disturbing philosophic/religious ideas of Swedenborg in the work of the Argentinian poet, even if at times they are not always in agreement with Borges.

Being, for Swedenborg, is one: the foundation of his system lies in 'the assertion of unity, as a condition that makes all reality possible'.[14] The division of being into stages, in turn, is explained by establishing an ontological union of the whole universe which is reflected in each and every part. On this point the Borgean Aleph is mirrored. For Swedenborg—as for Borges—the determination of the existence of everything (although this is not to evoke pantheism) involves a richness of plurality by virtue of the fact that 'everything is distinctly one'. Borges writes: 'I saw the Aleph, from every point, I saw the earth in the Aleph; and in the earth I saw the Aleph again and the earth in the Aleph'.[15] According to José Antonio Antón-Pacheco, this involves 'plural richness, metaphysic variety, a germinal capacity of being, and fructification', the fundamental forms of which are representations and the correspondences. However, where Borges veers away from the Mystic of the North is when the Mystic does not propose any great confusion of the concrete in the Absolute nor the dissolution of plurality in the abstract, i.e. the loss of ontological delimitation in the unknown Other.[16] Swedenborgian determination is, ultimately, the attempt to personify or personalise all things according to the parameters that shape and individualise their distinctive features.[17]

Another difference between Swedenborg and the neo-Platonic heritage of Borges is that for Swedenborg God is neither ineffable nor can he be defined as an imponderable abyss. According to Swedenborg, it is possible to talk about God in the configuration and determination of the primordial Man: the Grand Man (heaven itself, or the Pleroma); the Logos of Filon of Alexandria, which correspond to the Logos of man in created nature. This is why, in general, hell is the inability to be true to oneself; the refusal to 'develop with integrity, the spiritual possibilities of one's own human nature'. In short, it is to close one's interiors 'to the presence of the divine light'.[18] (Borges was very conscious of this and he let it be known in two verses of the aforementioned homonymous sonnet: 'I knew that the Glory and the Averno / in your soul are and its mythologies'.)[19] Here, the Swedish mystic also makes use of the 'extreme and exhaustive enumerations' that can be found in the parallels between man and the Grand Man—and we might refer also to 'The Aleph' or 'Mateo XXV, 30', among many others. Based on specific correspondences, these parallels show the indelible presence of the sacred in each element of God and man because the members and physical organs that are found in man are representations of the qualities of the divine.[20] From the perspective of this fantastic reading, it is possible to see the vision of the Aleph in the face and viscera in Borges the narrator, as well as the face and viscera of his readers. It is seen in the tears that are shed from the solemn and majestic recognition that the sacred is in himself and in the reader.

Maybe the most significant parallel between Borges and Swedenborg is the intermixture, common in mystical literature, of the concepts of space and time. Swedenborg noted in his *Conjugial Love* and *Divine Providence,* respectively, that 'there are no dimensional spaces in the spiritual world, but they have appearances of space, and these appearances are determined according to the states of their life, and their states of life are determined according to states of love' (CL §50) and that 'time is only an appearance according to the state of the affection from which thought springs' (DP §49).[21] Swedenborg sensed that both categories depend on man. In the ecstatic experience or celestial order, consciousness constructs its own time and space. Space turns into interior temporality which—in the spiritual realm—is qualitatively subordinated to the experience of spirit: 'the greater the love and wisdom, the closer one is drawn in love and understanding to the beloved object'.[22] *Ipso facto*, the narrator of 'The Aleph' has lost his beloved, Beatriz Viterbo, and moments before descending to see the mysterious and inexplicable object that Carlos Argentino jealousy guards in his cellar, he cannot repress an outburst of affection when he comes across a faded photograph, on top of a piano, of the young girl.[23] The narrator takes a few private moments to bring to mind the image of his beloved;

> No one could see us; in desperate tenderness I approached the portrait.
> "Beatriz, Beatriz Elena, Beatriz Elena Viterbo", I said, "Beloved Beatriz, Beatriz
> lost forever— it is me, it's me, Borges".

Then, alone, he goes down to the cellar, and with Beatriz as a guide, he sees the Aleph.

It is also worth stressing that this is not the whole picture. In the spiritual experiences of Swedenborg, time is rendered spatial and is expressed 'in terms and concepts of space, but everything occurs interiorly, as consciousness of time', whose movements are exposed in terms of duration.[24] Strictly speaking, the space/time categories are turned into affections of the soul symbolically codified:

> In this way, space is love, time is wisdom, colour is good, light is the truth of
> faith...[25]

The same also happens to Borges, the protagonist. When he enters the cellar, the vision of the Aleph dissolves his sense of space and time through an incessant series of antithetic relations. Time and place are vertiginously and simultaneously juxtaposed and super-imposed. Can it be said that the presence of Swedenborg here, in the work of Borges, is simply another playful whim of an *agnostótico* writer?[26] An affirmative answer to this question would seem indefensible: it is rather that the reciprocity between the mystic *in puribus* and the atypical religiosity of Swedenborg is revealed.

It is in support of these themes—and drawing on the mystical experiences underlying *Feeling in Death* and 'Mateo XXV, 30' respectively—that Borges feels confident to speak, with his typical non-challenge, on the polemical mysticism of his admired Swedenborg. Let us pause for a moment at the lecture of June 9th 1978 at the University of Belgrano, published in *Borges oral* (1979). Here, Borges not only condenses picturesque anecdotes of Swedenborg's biography, he also expounds those ideas of Swedenborg that have had a deep effect on his vision of life and literature. In Borges, there is a natural complement between the intensity of his mysticism and his aspiration to become a true *clásico*.[27]

What captivates Borges—more than that of Basilides or Valentino—is Swedenborg's heterodoxy. He speaks about the salvation of works that 'are not, [contained in religious] ceremonies or mass: but are true works, works in which the whole man is present, that is, in his spirit and, even more curiously, his intelligence'. [28] In the same way, Swedenborg's vision of personal immortality goes against the Christian belief of a perfect and luminous Paradise, where spiritual beings simply reside in the presence of the Father, the Son and the Holy Ghost. Swedenborg talks about death as a fact so natural, that it goes unnoticed by the individual because 'everything that surrounds him is the same' as in the material world, with the only difference that 'everything, in the other world, is more vivid than in this one'. The other side is more colourful, has clearer forms, and everything is shown to be more concrete: 'it is as if we [on this side] were living in the shadow'. Even sex is more intense. Borges' idea, taken from Saint Augustine's the *City of God,* is that 'sensual enjoyment is greater in Paradise than here, because it cannot be assumed that the fall has improved our lot'. [29] Swedenborg himself might have written those words. Borges also refers to the revelation received by Swedenborg in his *Dream Diary*: '[I was] in London, preceded by dreams [...] that were erotic'. [30] This passage outlines a crisis caused by dreams and visions, recorded—almost immediately after awakening—between the night of 24-25th of March until the night of 26-27th of October, 1744. Borges' allusion to the sexuality of Swedenborg's mystical marriage deserves careful commentary. It is an important allusion upon which he bases his esteem for the Swedish mystic.

In Swedenborg's *Diary*, both dreams and scientific work are interwoven in a figurative language. Attractive and repulsive women share his bed and are discussed as accurate/inaccurate themes of his empirical investigation which are then contextualised in a theosophical exegesis. At §§52-54, he writes of the famous vision of Christ (occurring during the night of the 6-7th of April) that will mark him forever. [31] In many respects, his language is consistent with the universal language of mysticism: it evokes temporal imprecision (as in the *Memorial* of Pascal) i.e. 'about twelve o'clock or perhaps it was at one or two in the morning'; he writes of being shaken by a sudden unexpected intensity i.e. 'such a strong shivering seized me, from my head to my feet, as a thunder produced by several clouds colliding'; he also acknowledges the ineffability of the experience, of it 'shaking me beyond description'; and he recognises his own insurmountable subjection to the divinity when he describes himself as being 'clearly awake' and yet seeing 'how I was overthrown'.

Likewise, the subject is both surprised and ignorant *ab initio* as to what has happened to him and why: 'I wondered' he writes, 'what this was supposed to mean'. He is stricken with an impotent voice and points to a glossalalia, or speaking with tongues: 'I spoke as if awake but found that the words were put into my mouth'. A third hand—the hand of Christ—intervenes with a firm grasp to dispel fears and doubts, whilst also inspiring confidence. Then, the realisation occurs: Swedenborg is in the lap of Christ. The face he is contemplating has an undeniable bearing of ineffable saintliness. The unique beauty of that smiling face—in the way that Saint Catherine of Siena had also seen it—inspires in Swedenborg the extraordinary assertion that this is the face of Christ as when alive as a man among men. 'He was smiling at me,' he writes, 'and I was convinced that he looked like this when he was alive'. Finally, there is a request of a health certificate, i.e. 'He spoke to me and asked if I have a health certificate', which Swedenborg interprets as a call to his theosophic-scientific mission: 'He said, "Well then, do!"'—that is, as I inwardly grasped this, "Do love me" or "Do as promised"'. Lars Berquist suggests that, in the context of the *Diary*, this demand is for an evidence of health in a moral sense i.e.:

> [that] from Swedenborg's point of view, a certificate of sanity surely meant mastery of temptation and implied a mobilisation of his own will to turn toward God completely and submit fully. [32]

This experience of Christ, in fact, is the axis of the entire 'mystical marriage' of Swedenborg which because of its realism can be distinguished from traditional accounts. However, in order to understand—from the exact co-ordinates of the *Diary*—the explicit examples of eroticism in his mysticism, it is better to study the visions of the night between the 9-10th of April (§87 and §88). [33] Experiencing a state of beatitude, an 'inward joy that could be felt all over the body', Swedenborg becomes aware of the concentric and interior nature of the mystical phenomenon:

> Everything seemed in a consummate way to be fulfilled, flew upwards as it were,

concealing itself in something infinite, as a centre, where love itself was, and it seemed as if it issued thence round about and then down again, thus moving around in incomprehensible circles from the centre that is love, and back.

From here, and given his concept of unity as a final period of the evolution of everything created, and his eagerness to harmonise the soul with the body, Swedenborg speaks of marital love in exactly the same terms as his exegesis of the nuptial mysticism:

This love, which then filled me, in a mortal body is like the delight a chaste man enjoys when he really is in love and makes love to his spouse. Such an extreme joy was suffused over my whole body, and this for a long while.

Imitating the language of commentators like Saint Bernardo Origins to the *Song of Songs*, Swedenborg's description compares favourably with Christian orthodoxy; however, when it is his turn to narrate examples of the *mystica unio* in his visions, he makes use of a simple and scientific language whilst keeping meaning multiple:

120: I lay with one who was not beautiful, but whom I liked. She had what others have, and there I touched her; but in front, there seem to be some set of teeth; it appeared to be Archenholtz [Arckenholtz] in a woman's shape. What this means I don't know, perhaps that I should not touch any woman or get deeply involved in politics or something like that.

171: Throughout the night, something was dictated to me, something holy, which ended with *sacrarium et sanctuarium*. I found myself in bed with one. She said: if you had not said *sanctuarium*, we would do it. I turned away from her; with her hand, she touched me and it got big, bigger than ever. I turned around and applied it; it bent, yet it went in. She said it was long. Meanwhile, I thought that a child must come out of this, and I got off *en merville*.[34]

At §120, the inconceivable teeth of the vagina responds to a *caveat* of compromising matters, or a warning of difficult loves and risky consummations, which might be exampled in the activities of certain characters of the Swedish politics (i.e. of Johan Arckenholtz, a historian and politician, who opposed the alliance between Sweden with France). On the other hand, the hermeneutic or interpretation of section §171 is found in the following paragraph, where, regardless of the political and scientific context, the dreamer declares his passion for God and his longing for knowledge:

> 172: This signifies the utmost love of the Holy One, for all love originates from that source, constituting a series, in the body manifest in its seminal projection; and when the ejaculation is there and is pure, it answers to the love of wisdom [. . .]

Such use of scientific language, in order to characterise the mystical phenomenon, must have dazzled the clever Borges, who was inclined to surprise his readers with cunning sentences and linguistic juggling. It is exactly this functional use of language that is reflected in Borges' commentaries on the eschatology of Swedenborg, and from which he makes aesthetic use as well.

The paradise of Swedenborg has another feature particular to the narratives of Borges. Unknown to man, both angels and demons compete to gain access to the recently deceased by speaking with him in the spiritual realm, the transitional sphere between the heavens and the hells. Each man has to decide if he will become an angel or a demon according to the conversation that he likes the most, or the conversation that corresponds most closely to his angelic or demonic temperament. God does not, as such, condemn anyone to hell: it is the person who decides. Some become demons because they are attracted to the demoniac reasoning in accord with the desires that have dominated their life.[35] Both heaven and hell, as such, are peopled by those who have chosen to be there: neither are the product of the righteous hand of God. In addition, there are some who seek Paradise with a wrong idea as to what goes on there:

> They think that in heaven they will pray continuously; and they are allowed to do so, but within a few days or weeks they become tired: they realise that this is not heaven. Then they flatter God; they praise him. But God does not need adulation.

And so these people also become tired of flattering God. Then they think they will be happy speaking with loved ones; and after some time they understand that their loved ones and illustrious heroes are as tedious in the other life as in this one. So they become tired of that and then get on with the true work of heaven.

[. . .] Swedenborg's heaven is a heaven of love and, above all, a heaven of work, an altruistic heaven. Each angel works for all others; and all others work for each other. It is not a passive heaven, and nor does it involve recompense. If one has an angelic temperament then one will go to a heaven where one is comfortable. But there is also difference that is very important in Swedenborg's heaven: his heaven is eminently intellectual.

[. . .] This is an innovation of Swedenborg. It is thought that salvation is ethical in nature. It is understandable that if a man is fair, he is saved. Jesus said, 'The kingdom of heaven is for the poor'. But Swedenborg goes further. He says that this is not enough, and that man must also be saved intellectually. He imagines heaven, above all, as a series of theological conversations between angels. And if a man cannot follow those conversations he is unworthy. [36]

The parallel with 'The Circular ruins' is evident, although not a copy of Swedenborg's doctrine because Buddhist content also emerges. In the circular amphitheatre 'that was, in a certain way, a burned down temple', the dreamed dreamer dictates lessons to those faces 'that were trying to respond with understanding, as if they were guessing the importance of the exam, which would redeem one of them of his condition of vain appearance and would interpolate him in the real world'. The soul that excels in intelligence and cleverness over others will deserve redemption, and will re-emerge 'to participate in the universe'. [37] But there is more. To this second kind of intellectual salvation—surely an addenda by Swedenborg to the ethics of Jesus—Borges points to a third, supplied by William Blake, of an art-form based on the parables of Christ, an oral literature accessible to all listeners. Here, one is obliged to evoke Schopenhauer, but Borges opts for Blake, whose mysticism, even today, continues to encourage ardent debates. Borges recognises that the mystic sensibility of Blake clarifies many of Swedenborg's uncomfortable sentences. For instance, 'The fool shall not enter into Glory, no matter how holy he may be', or this one that is even harder 'Strip yourselves of sanctity and clothe yourselves in intelligence'.[38] Such paradoxes could only have captivated the fabulator of 'The Aleph', who was so intentionally contradictory in the academic exposition of his philosophic and aesthetic ideas.

This prudence, also, made Swedenborg Borges' favourite mystic. 'He does not preach', he says of Swedenborg, 'he published his books anonymously in a sober and dry Latin'. Borges also admires Swedenborg's tolerance of Buddhist resonance: 'His servants [. . .] used to see him conversing with angels or arguing with demons. In such dialogues he never imposed his own ideas'. Even more, the Argentinian poet deeply respects and emulates the Swedish mystic's reservations: 'Of course, he did not allow others to mock of his visions; but neither did he desire to force them: instead he would divert the conversation away from such themes'.[39] It also reveals the key for Borges' tolerance of Buddhism and his modesty when faced with enquiries—one might think of W Barnstone and L López-Baralt—who tried to access the silence of his own mystical experiences. The mystical condition *in puribus,* therefore—although expressible—impelled him to modesty, because he recognised himself as a writer of the world and indifferent to any mystical behaviour that might be questionable to him in academic circles. Nevertheless, his understanding of mystical phenomenon can still astonish the reader that goes behind these traces. First, Borges vindicates the authenticity of Swedenborg's mysticism by negating the claims of madness voiced by Swedenborg's contemporaries with regard to the stranger Swedenborg saw in the street and which he identified as Jesus. According to Borges, a mystic never loses his sanity. And Borges emphasises this about Swedenborg with irrefutable certainty. The claim of insanity, Borges states:

is negated by the clarity of his work, by the fact that we never feel we are in the presence of a madman. When revealing his doctrine he always writes with great clarity. [. . .] And that work is very vast, written in a very quiet style [. . .] Swedenborg reveals everything with authority, with quiet authority.[40]

Second, Borges also draws attention to the self confessed admiration of Swedenborg by Henry James Snr: 'I know that William and Henry James' father was a Swedenborgian'. He also identifies Swedenborg's followers in North America and deplores the inexcusable exclusion of those texts in Christian bookshops:

> I have found Swedenborgians in the United States, where there is a society that is still publishing his books and translating them into English. [...][41]
>
> But in some theosophic bookshops we can find no works by Swedenborg. And yet, he is a mystic more much complex than others; others simply tell us that they have experienced ecstasy, or they try to describe this ecstasy in a literary way. Swedenborg is the first explorer of the other world, an explorer that we should take seriously. [42]

Third, Borges establishes an importance between the mystic who writes poetry and the poet who imitates mystical language. He takes, for example, the Italian poet of Christianity:

> In the case of Dante, [for instance] who also offers to us a description of the Hell, Purgatory and Paradise, we understand as literary fiction. We do not really believe that everything said refers to personal experience. Besides, he is constrained by the verse: he could not have experienced the verse. [43]

In reality, the problem is not poetry, the literary gender of the metaphor or the hyperbole for excellence. The conflict is rather that most cultures privilege a poetic expression of the nuptial mysticism. Borges, in contrast, decisively, distances himself from this. He opts for a 'serene prose', the 'prose' of Swedenborg 'that is above all lucid, and without metaphor and exaggeration'.

To conclude therefore: the two spiritual experiences of Borges—the mystical raptures of 1928 and, later, of 1951-53—do more than inspire him as a writer of stories and poems. They throw light on his ability to subscribe to the doctrines and heterodoxies of mysticism itself within the context of natural mysticism. Without these experiences it would have been impossible for Borges to offer a transcendental response to the supernatural proposals of the Swedish mystic. Those experiences enabled him to both read and understand the thrilling revelation of angelic communion and the reality of the Grand Man that breathes depth into the soul of mankind. What is left to say, finally, is that it would seem acceptable to assume a universality of mystical phenomenon, and that variations and contrasts between individuals can be ascribed to the cultural framework in which they occur. The contrasts between the Mystic of the North and the mystic *in puribus* in this sense, therefore, respond to the context and aspirations of the will of each individual, according to the results of their extraordinary experiences evidenced in their productive lives.

NOTES

[1] Blaise Pascal, *Pensées de Blaise Pascal*, edited by Zacharie Tourneur, (Paris, Librairie Philosophique J Vrin, 1942), 19. His volume is one of the few publications of Pascal's work that contains a copy of the *Memorial*, the original of which is lost. See my comment in *Boletin de la Academia Puertorriquena de la Lengua Espanola*, (San Juan, Plaza Mayor, 1999), 88-91.

[2] Lars Berquist makes this clear at the beginning of his introduction to the commentary of this text when he writes: 'Since we cannot ask Swedenborg himself, we must penetrate the actual wording of the texts, especially since *he never commented upon them and never intended them for publication*', (my emphasis). *Swedenborg's Dream Diary*, (USA: Swedenborg Foundation, 2001), 3.

[3] The works of the famous American philosopher and psychologist William James (1842-1910) considerably expand the optic of the mystical phenomenon in the non-religious context. James' main contribution can be found in his book *The Varieties of Religious Experience: A Study in Human Nature* (1902) which documents countless testimonies of people who are non-religious and even non-believers, who describe experiences with irrefutable mystical content and origin. On the other hand, the German theologian Karl Rahner (1904-84) has systemised new mystical experiences discussing the capacity of the ordinary man to make all aspects of

himself divine *hic et nunc* by means of grace. Because the mystical experience is shared equally between the religious and the non-religious (including atheists), the model of the traditional mystic—usually defined according to the religious medieval archetype—has given space to a natural mysticism, adopted by postmodernism as a result of the secularisation of modern culture. For further study of this phenomenon and the subject of natural mysticism, see my article: 'Del santo deshumanizado al hombre santificado: el arquetipo medieval religioso da paso al místico natural de la modernidad' ['From the dehumanised saint to the sanctified man: the religious medieval archetype gives way to the natural mystic of the modernity'], in my study *Jorge Luis Borges o el (re)negado místico: hacia el rescate de sus dos encuentros con la eternidad* [*Jorge Luis Borges or the (re)negated mystic: to the rescue of his two encounters with eternity*] (Investigation Work, presented to the Department of Integrated Philology, in the area of Latin-American Literature, at the University of Seville, 2003), 70-81. It is from these co-ordinates that Borges, the meticulous reader of William James, did not hesitate to describe his two experiences as mystical whenever urged to speak on it, either by his own initiative or for the insistence of his audience. I will explore this point in more depth later.

[4] See my study *Jorge Luis Borges o el (re)negado místico:...* [Jorge Luis Borges or the (re)negated mystic...], 104-108.

[5] Juan Arana, *La eternidad de lo efímero. Ensayos sobre Jorge Luis Borges,* [The Eternity of the Ephemera: Essays on Jorge Luis Borges], (Madrid, Blblioteca Nueva, 2000), 111.

[6] One can read a detailed commentary to this poem in my study *Jorge Luis Borges o el (re)negado místico:...* [Jorge Luis Borges or the (re)negated mystic...], 108-117. See, also, an important essay by Luce López-Baralt entitled 'Borges y William James: el problema de la expresión del fenómeno místico' ['Borges and William James: the problem of the expression of the mystical phenomena'], edited by Alfonso de Toro and Fernando de Toro in *El siglo de Borges (1). Retrospetiva-Presente-Futoro* [The Century of Borges (I). Retrospective-Present-Future] (Madrid, *Iberoamericana*, Number 17), 29-70.

[7] In his interview 'The Secret Islands'. *Borges at Eighty*, (Indiana, Indiana University Press), 10-11.

[8] López-Baralt insisted that Borges shared the details of his two 'mystical' experiences but he received the following vague response: 'If you write about St John of the Cross, you simply know that I cannot answer you. Those experiences are inexpressible'. See L López-Baralt and Emilio R Báez-Rivera, '¿Vivió Jorge Luis Borges la experiencia mística del Aleph? Entrevista a Maria Kodama de Borges' ['Did Jorge Luis Borges live the mystical experience of the *Aleph*? Interview to Maria Kodama of Borges'], in L López-Baralt and Lorenzo Piera (eds.) *El sol a medianoche. La experiencia mítica: tradicíon y actualidad* [The Sun in Midnight. The Mystical Experience: Tradition and Actuality], (Madrid, Trotta), 252; and also in López-Baralt, 'Borges o la mística del silencio: lo que había al otro lado del Zahir' ['Borges or the mystic of the silence: what there was on the other side of the Zahir'], in Alfonso de Toro and Fernando de

Toro [eds.], *Jorge Luis Borges. Pensamiento y saber en el siglo XX,* [Jorge Luis Borges. Thought and knowledge in the Twentieth Century], (Madrid, Iberoamericana, Number.16), 56.

[9] See the interview by L López-Baralt and Báez-Rivera, '¿Vivió Jorge Luis Borges la experiencia mística del Aleph?' ['Did Jorge Luis Borges live the mystical experience of the Aleph? Interview to Maria Kodama of Borges']. *ibid.*, 256-259.

[10] José Antonio Antón-Pacheco, 'El centario del nacimiento de Jorge Luis Borges' ['The Centenary of Jorge Luis Borges's birth'] in *Letra y Espiritu* [Letter and Spirit], Number 6, 51.

[11] J L Borges, *Obras completas* [Complete works] (1923-1972), (Emecé, Buenos Aires), 704. This is not the last time that Borges dismisses the validity of the supernatural experiences of *bona fide* mystics. In the interview with Willis Barnstone ('The Secret Islands', 11) he negated the authenticity of the mysticism of Fray Luis de León as well as the mysticism of San Juan de la Cruz and all of the Spanish mystics: 'I wonder if Fray Luis de León had any mystical experience? I would say not. When I talk of mystics, I think of Swedenborg, Angelus Silesius, as well as the Persians. But not the Spaniards. I don't think they had any mystical experiences [...] I think that Saint John of the Cross was following the pattern of the Song of Songs. And that's all. I suspect he never had any actual experience'. Maybe this is a joke...the certain thing is that Borges prefers to be located in the company of controversial mystics, i.e. in the company of the heterodox mystics of Christian tradition—with Swedenborg at its head—and the company of other cultural confessions, such as Sufism (in the possible hidden self-recognition of his own beliefs) which, according to the theologians, philosophers and experts of mystical theism, can only fit into the parameters of a natural mysticism.

[12] Borges, *Obras completas* [Complete works], 909.

[13] *Ibid.*, 936.

[14] José Antonio Antón-Pacheco, *Un Libro sobre Swedenborg* [A book about Swedenborg], (University of Seville, Seville, 1991), 15. English version pubished by Arcana Books, (USA, South Carolina, 2000).

[15] Borges, 'The Aleph', *Obras completas* [Complete works], 626.

[16] Antón-Pacheco, *Un Libro sobre Swedenborg*, 17-22.

[17] 'A person is more differentiated than a stone, and possesses more individual traits. Consequently, a person has greater ontological density than a stone. Accordingly we see the relevent role played by man, and, more concretely, by angels, since we may consider the figure of the angel is nothing more than the maximum prototype of personalisation, i.e., determination: the angel is the realisation of man's ontological and existential potential' (Antón-Pacheco. *Un Libro sobre Swedenborg*, 23). The man who is able to fulfill all his possibilities will become—according to Swedenborg—an angel.

[18] *Ibid.*, 40.

[19] Borges, 'Emanuel Swedenborg', *Obras completas* [Complete works], 909.

[20] In another note, Antón-Pacheco cites a fragment of Swedenborg directly:

'The universal heaven is so formed as to correspond to the Lord, to His Divine Humanity; and...man is so formed as to correspond to heaven with regard to each and all things in him, and through heaven to the Lord' (*Arcana Caelestia* §3624). 'It is from this ground that it has been occasionally said above, in speaking of heaven and angelic societies, that they belong to some province of the body; as that of the head, or that of the breast, or of the abdomen, or of some member or organ therein; and this because of the correspondence here spoken of' (*Arcana Caelestia* §3625).

[21] Cited by Antón-Pacheco, *Ibid.*, 59.

[22] *Ibid.*, 60.

[23] Borges, 'The Aleph', *Obras completas* [Complete works], 624

[24] Antón-Pacheco, *Un Libro sobre Swedenborg* [A book about Swedenborg], 61.

[25] *Ibid.*, 60.

[26] This adjectival form has its root in the term *agnostoteísmo*, coined by Julián Velarde to properly denote those who, starting from Kant, affirm that God cannot be known, we can only believe in Him. (*El agnosticismo* [Agnosticism], Madrid, Trotta, 1996), 21, 53. In this way, Valerde distinguishes with precision the voice of 'agnosticism' in the light of the original proposal of Thomas H Huxley (*El agnosticismo* [Agnosticism], 11).

[27] In this way is expressed a sagacious observation by Maria Caballero Wangüemert: '[...] if in the seventies Borges bears a view that supports him not simply a *canónico* Argentinian author, but as one of the great writers of all the times, then the eighties and the nineties contemplate an overwhelming list of studies that make up an image closer to the concept of *clásico*'. *Borges y la crítica. El nacimiento de un clásico* [Borges and the Critic. The birth of a classic], (Complutense, Madrid, 1999), 173.

[28] Borges, 'Emanuel Swedenborg', *Borges Oral*, (Madrid, Alianza, 1998), 43.

[29] *Ibid.*, 46-48.

[30] *Ibid.*, 45. This is the only time Borges speaks about the *Dream Diary* of Swedenborg; but those who know the literary work of Borges will know that, in his silences, there is hidden a sea of incognitos which have significant repercussion on his intellectual universe.

[31] *Swedenborg's Dream Diary*, 126.

[32] *Ibid.*, 127.

[33] *Ibid.*, 154-155.

[34] *Ibid.*, 180, 211.

[35] Borges, 'Emanuel Swedenborg', 54.

[36] *Ibid.*, 52-4.

[37] Borges, *Obras completas* [Complete works], 452.

[38] Cited by Borges, 'Emanuel Swedenborg', 54.

[39] *Ibid.*, 55-6.

[40] *Ibid.*, 45-6.

[41] *Ibid.*, 59.

[42] *Ibid.*, 60.

[43] *Ibid.*, 60.

Biographies

Index

Biographies

Jorge Luis Borges is regarded as one of the greatest writers of the 20th century. His most well known works in English are *Labyrinths* (containing *Fictions* and other prose poems), *The Aleph, A Universal History of Infamy* and *The Book of Sand*. Born in Buenos Aires, in 1899, he co-founded the journals *Proa* and *Sur,* and worked as a literary advisor to the publishing house Emecé Editores. From the late 1930s to 1946 he was first assistant at the Miguel Cane branch of the Buenos Aires Municipal Library and later became Director of the National Library (1955-73). As an essayist he published *Discusión* (1932), *Historia de la Eternidad* (1936) and *Otras Inquisiciones* (1952). His influences include the Cabbala, Swedenborg, George Berkeley and other figures of the Idealist tradition. He was awarded the International Publishers Prize with Samuel Beckett in 1961. Works such as *El Jardín de Senderos que se bifurcan* (1941), *Ficciónes* (1944) and *El Aleph* (1949) were translated into English and international recognition followed. Practically blind in later years, Borges nevertheless published *El libro de los Seres Imaginarios* (1967), *El Informe de Brodie* (1970) and *El libro de arena* (1975). He died in Geneva in 1986.

Robert and *Elizabeth Barrett Browning* were English poets of considerable note, and

---

like Samuel Taylor Coleridge, were close friends of the Swedenborgian Charles Augustus Tulk. Elizabeth was born in Durham, in 1806. She mastered Greek, Latin and several modern languages by the age of thirteen. At the age of nine she fell off a pony, suffering a spinal injury, and was thereafter prone to illness. 'Battle of Marathon', written when she was twelve, was published privately by her father in 1820. *An Essay on the Mind and Other Poems* (1826) and *Prometheus Unbound* (1833) followed. The family were forced to sell their Herefordshire home in 1827 and settled at Wimpole Street, London. It was here that she first met Robert Browning, who had corresponded with her after admiring her *Poems* (1844). They married secretly in 1846 and moved to Italy where her health improved and she wrote *Sonnets from the Portuguese* (1847) and *Aurora Leigh* (1857). Robert was born in Camberwell in 1812. He briefly attended the newly opened London University, but most of his extensive learning was self-taught from his father's 6,000 volume library. Among his works are *Paracelsus* (1835), *Sordello* (1840), *Pippa Passes* (1841), *The Pied Piper of Hamelin* (1842) and *Dramatis Personae* (1864). It was after Elizabeth's death, in 1861, that he began to receive international recognition as a poet, notably with *The Ring and the Book* (1869). He died in Venice, in 1889, and is buried in Poets' Corner, Westminster Abbey.

Samuel Taylor Coleridge is perhaps the most influential English poet and writer of the Romantic period. He was born in Ottery St Mary in 1772 and studied at Cambridge University. In 1795 he published *Poems on Various Subjects* which was followed by *Poems*. He was introduced to William Wordsworth and the pair published *Lyrical Ballads* in 1798. Opening with Coleridge's 'The Rime of the Ancient Mariner' and closing with Wordsworth's 'Tintern Abbey', *Lyrical Ballads* effectively started the English Romantic movement. In 1798-9, he visited Germany with William and Dorothy Wordsworth, and discovered the writings of Kant and Schelling and began a translation of Schiller's *Wallenstein* trilogy. From 1808-18 he gave a series of lectures (mostly in London) that earned him the title of the greatest Shakespearean critic. In 1809 he set up the literary and political periodical *The Friend*. 1816 marked the publication of the unfinished poems 'Kubla Khan' and 'Christabel'. *Biographia Literaria* (1817), a twenty-five chapter work of autobiographical notes and dissertations on many subjects, brought together much of

Coleridge's literary theory and criticism. In 1816, trying to free himself from the grasp of an opium addiction, he took refuge at the Highgate home of Dr James Gillman. In 1817 Coleridge was introduced to Charles Augustus Tulk and the works of Swedenborg and, from hereon, he devoted himself to theological and socio-political works, including *Aids to Reflection* (1825) and *Church and State* (1830). Coleridge died in Highgate in 1834.

Ralph Waldo Emerson, widely regarded as the most significant essayist and poet of the American Transcendental movement and a key spokesman for the abolition of slavery, was born in Boston in 1803, the son of a clergyman. He studied at Harvard College and Harvard Divinity School—where he first encountered the works of Swedenborg—before becoming a pastor at the Second Unitarian Church of Boston. A subsequent estrangement from organised religion, stemming from the death of his young wife, Ellen Tucker, led to his resignation three years later. After travelling to Europe in 1832, where he met William Wordsworth, Samuel Taylor Coleridge and Thomas Carlyle, Emerson returned to America, married Lydia Jackson and settled in the village of Concord, Massachussetts. In 1844 he gave his 'Emancipation in the British West Indies' address and in 1852 he spoke out against the Fugitive Slave Law. His works include *Nature* (1836), *Essays* (1842), *Essays: Second Series* (1844), *Representative Men* (1850), which includes his famous essay on Swedenborg, *English Traits* (1856) and *May-Day and Other Pieces* (1867). His essays and poems have influenced writers as diverse as Henry David Thoreau, Walt Whitman, Herman Melville, Nathaniel Hawthorne and Friedrich Nietzsche. He died in Concord in 1882.

August Strindberg, renowned Swedish novelist and playwright, was born in Stockholm in 1849 and studied at Uppsala University. He started his career as a journalist and a librarian before his literary breakthrough occurred with the novel *Röda Rummel* (*The Red Room*) in 1879. Strindberg married the Baroness Siri von Essen in 1877, the first of three marriages that would end unhappily. Strindberg received some notoriety through his collection of stories *Giftas* (*Marrying*) in 1884 and he was unsuccessfully prosecuted for his portrayal of the Last Supper in the novella *The Reward of Virtue* (1884). 1895 marked the start of Strindberg's 'Inferno' period, where he developed an interest in alchemy and Swedenborg. This was to be the basis for his novels *Inferno* in 1897 and *Legends* in

1898. In 1897 he began the *Till Damaskus* (*To Damascus*) trilogy which was finished in 1901. Strindberg wrote over seventy plays as well as novels, short stories and studies of Swedish History. His most famous works include *Fadren* (*The Father*), *Fröken Julie* (*Miss Julie*) and *Ett Drömspel* (*A Dream Play*). His influence is far-reaching and can be seen in Eugène Ionesco, Harold Pinter, Samuel Beckett and Eugene O'Neill. He died in the Blue Tower, Stockholm, in 1912.

Charles Augustus Tulk (1786-1849) was the son of John Augustus Tulk, one of the founders of the New Jerusalem Church, which held its first conference (attended by William Blake and his wife) in Great East Cheap, London in April 1789. With his father and others, Tulk was a founder in 1810 of the Swedenborg Society and was its chairman for a number of years. The artist John Flaxman (another founder member of the Society) was a family friend. Flaxman introduced Tulk to William Blake (he was later to become one of his patrons) and in 1817 he met Samuel Taylor Coleridge. He lent Blake's poems to Coleridge and later introduced the two poets to each other. In 1820 Tulk entered Parliament and was later a founder member and 'Proprietor' of London University (now University College London). He became a close friend and associate of the radical leader, Joseph Hume, whose daughter Mary Catherine Hume was to write his biography. Towards the end of his life Tulk made an extended visit to Florence. He was already acquainted with Elizabeth Barrett Browning and here he introduced Elizabeth and her husband to Swedenborg's great work on the spiritual nature of sex and marriage, *Conjugial Love*. Tulk's 'idealistic' interpretation of Swedenborg's theology, set out particularly in his book *Spiritual Christianity*, found little favour with his fellow Swedenborgians, but was praised in the *Massachusetts Quarterly Review*, of which Emerson was joint editor, as the only 'rational reproduction' of Swedenborg's theology. The later 'idealistic' interpretation of Swedenborg by Henry James Snr in *The Secret of Swedenborg* and other works was perhaps influenced by Tulk's views, Tulk being a colleague in the Swedenborg Society of James's later friend James John Garth Wilkinson.

Walt Whitman, along with Emerson, is generally regarded as one of America's greatest poets. Born in Long Island, New York in 1819, he left school early to help support his family and worked as a printer's apprentice. He also worked as a teacher, carpenter and journalist, writing and editing for several periodicals including *The Brooklyn Eagle* (1840-8) and *The Brooklyn Times* (1857-8). In 1855 Whitman published the first edition of his classic *Leaves of Grass*. He was to revise, add to and reissue the work constantly, with eight editions being published during his lifetime. The book was a commercial failure and criticised for its style and sexual content but nevertheless attracted the praise of Ralph Waldo Emerson. During the Civil War, which broke out in 1861, Whitman worked as a volunteer nurse and later as a clerk in the Department of the Interior, a post which he was dismissed from because his boss thought *Leaves of Grass* an immoral book. Whitman's poetry, written in free verse, with a disregard to metre, depicted the horrors and neglect of the human condition, whilst also celebrating democracy and the freedom and dignity of the individual. Other works includes *Drum-Taps* (1865), *Sequel to Drum Taps* (1865-6), *Democratic Vistas* (1871) and *November Boughs* (1888). Whitman died in Camden, New Jersey in 1892 after preparing a 'deathbed' edition of his masterpiece, *Leaves of Grass*. Whitman's influence can be seen on many American writers including Henry Miller, Allen Ginsberg and Jack Kerouac.

Index